REMEMBERING

MEDINA
COUNTY

REMEMBERING

MEDINA
COUNTY

TALES FROM OHIO'S WESTERN RESERVE

JUDY A. TOTTS

Charleston · London

THE
History
PRESS

Published by The History Press
Charleston, SC 29403
www.historypress.net

Cover design by Natasha Momberger

First published 2009

Manufactured in the United States

ISBN 978.1.59629.617.6

Library of Congress Cataloging-in-Publication Data

Totts, Judy A.
Remembering Medina County : tales from Ohio's Western Reserve / Judy A. Totts.
p. cm.
Includes bibliographical references.
ISBN 978-1-59629-617-6
1. Medina County (Ohio)--History. 2. Medina County (Ohio)--Biography. 3. Frontier
and pioneer life--Ohio--Medina County. 4. Western Reserve (Ohio)--History. I. Title.
F497.M5T68 2008
977.1'35--dc22
2008046950

Contents

INTRODUCTION

How often do we gaze deeply at the ordinary, the places and the people around us, and allow them to become part of us, to sink into our hearts? That includes the unseen as well, the history of our houses and our land. We exist like the growth rings of a tree, separate but part of a greater whole surrounding the heartwood that sprang up before Native Americans walked the forest paths, before ox carts and plowed fields, before the petals of our family stories get pressed between the pages of county history. Those who recently moved in still exist at the outer ring of the county, and, truth be told, the surface has changed enough over the years that parts of it seem new even to those of us who have been around a while.

Memory allows us to be a little closer to the beginning, like the summer sounds of childhood, hearing the A.I. Root Company whistle or the clang of the interurban bells that interrupted the clip-clop of hoofbeats around the square and the quiet countryside stretching to Chippewa Lake.

Newcomers don't remember Dr. Mansell's office next to the library or the X-ray machine in Griesinger's shoe store, where we could see the shadow of flesh surrounding the bones of our feet. Couples walked past the fountain in the square, where goldfish dodged the pennies the kids pitched at them. I can remember the scent of leaf smoke every fall and burn barrels in the backyards.

When we lived out of the county for six years, I took all that with me, even if I wasn't really aware of it. A lot had changed by the time we moved back. In swimming through the new depths, it was comforting to be able to touch bedrock at the bottom. Underneath, it was the same as it always had been—the history was still intact.

The park served as a favorite gathering place for people before evening band concerts.
Courtesy Medina County Historical Society.

Art teachers tell students that to develop their skills, they need to draw what they see, not what they think they see. This is true, too, of those memories that become the silent touchstones by which we measure other places we may live, looking at them without blinking, tracing their lines so we know them, even in the dark.

PART I

GLIMPSES: WHIRLWINDS, WHISKEY AND WEDDINGS

FRONTIER FAIRY TALES: FIRST WEDDINGS

The first birth, death and marriage in a new settlement are objects of considerable interest to the people. The first-born in a neighborhood grows up an individual of great importance; the first wedding is an event that is long-remembered, while the first funeral and the first grave in a lonely wilderness engender sad and mournful reflections that shadow the community for years.
—History of Medina County and Ohio

Long ago—perhaps not long enough to be considered once upon a time, but far enough removed from today as to have a fairy tale ambiance—travelers packed saddlebags with food, mounted their sturdy-limbed horses and left their villages with the rising sun at their backs.

When the road ended, they reined their animals onto deer trails that wandered through stands of slippery elm, oak and maple. They splashed through rising creek waters and turned their collars against cold spring winds. And every evening they huddled around their cooking fires and talked about places where wolves' eyes blinked and burned like yellow stars in dark pine groves. They craved those secret fields known only to soft-footed foxes and equally soft-footed hunters.

They were not royalty, but they dreamed like princes—not of castles, but of cabins, cattle and wheat fields—the kingdoms to be won from the wilderness south and west of the crooked river, the Cuyahoga. With the simple magic of names and sweat, they cast their spells of civilization. It wasn't long before families followed. And the country princes scythed the brambles and briar roses to reach the fair-haired daughters at church services who looked at them sideways and leaned on their hoes in the garden patch whenever the young men rode by.

Families passed many evenings reading or writing letters. Women of the household may have used the time to record births, marriages and deaths in the family Bible. *Courtesy Medina County Historical Society.*

Mothers opened the big Bibles in the parlors and entered names and wedding days. Township "firsts" were cause for celebration and fodder for historians:

> *The first couple married in the township* [Medina] *was Giles Barnes and Elizabeth Northrop on the 23rd of March, 1818. It was a time of great rejoicing, and the whole neighborhood turned out en masse to celebrate. Invitations had been sent out to all the dwellers in the township to attend. Their ceremony was performed by Rev. R. Searle, an Episcopal clergyman, and the first preacher in the township. The festivities were continued to a late hour; but as "the boys" had provided a good supply of torch bark, when the ceremonies and rejoicings were over, they went to their homes, lighted on their way by their bark torches. Some were said to have been a little "high" from the effects of the wine they had drank. This, however, was not considered in the least extraordinary (even for some clergymen at that day) under such circumstances as a frontier wedding. Whisky* [sic] *did not contain so much poison then as at the present day, hence was not so dangerous.*

In Guilford Township, Abigail Porter married David Wilson on December 18, 1818, at Lyman Munson's house in Seville, with wedding guests from Brunswick, Medina, Wadsworth and Mogadore.

The bride's "little dressing room was partitioned off from the rest of the house by quilts. She wore a steel-colored silk dress, her hair in finger-puffs, and she looked charming." Esquire Warner of Wadsworth officiated, and after the ceremony the couple rode to their own home on one horse.

"Although Mr. Wilson had scarcely anything in the world, except some new land, his ax and a horse, yet this brave girl united her destinies with his, well-knowing that if ever they had a comfortable home of their own, by their united toil they must make it. And this they did, though many were their discouragements, and in that home they lived happily together for almost half a century."

OLD GRAVEYARDS

Old graveyards are best for long, thoughtful walks. They're just a little wild, surrounded by slightly listing wrought-iron fences. Their stones are the color of moonlight through clouds, their edges worn by the thumbs of wind and rain, like coins tumbled in the pockets of storms. Small change for eternity.

Cold as a starless December night to touch, the oldest markers lean, as if propped by invisible canes, pawns and queens and kings all, ranged on a chess board of quiet stories.

Some newer cemeteries lie flat-faced, markers flush against the ground like steppingstones. Alike as cookie-cutter houses in a development, you have to know chapter and verse, column and row, to find your grandfather's bones, the script of your mother's name.

D.S. Longacre's horse-drawn hearse makes its way to the graveyard. Many Medina County pioneers were laid to rest in the cemetery next to St. Paul's Episcopal Church. *Courtesy John Gladden.*

The old stones—sculpted like angels and lambs, obelisks, with sturdy sentiments cut in broad-backed granite—struggle to remain upright against time and vandals. Like the individuals whose graves they mark, they do not easily lie down. Those who were the first to die in each township probably do not think much of the honor. I'd like to think they'd much rather their epitaphs remind the early mourners and, in years to come, people kneeling with paper and chalk to make rubbings of the stones, that once they loved to hold their children close, or often walked the banks of the Black River, like Katy Davis.

Katy drowned March 2, 1824, while attempting to cross the Black River by walking on a log. She was "a beautiful girl of 16 and loved by all." Her parents buried her in Harrisville because no official cemetery existed in Spencer Township, where she lived.

Stephen Harrington became the first person buried in Spencer, in 1826, on land belonging to Lynzey Bennett. The coffin was made of boards brought into the township in 1823 by John P. Marsh.

When Jane Strait, thirteen, daughter of Asa Strait, died in Litchfield Township, her funeral was the first open religious service held there. Her father opened his Bible and spoke the words over her grave.

The first stones did not stand lonely for long, because settlers faced uncertain medical treatment and diseases with names like "erysipalatus fever, which struck the township [Wadsworth] in 1844 and 1848…fatalities reached about 20 percent of those afflicted. Apparently the survivors lived in spite of, rather than because of, the blood-lettings they were subjected to as a cure. Dr. C.N. Lyman, son of Captain George Lyman, recalled that 'some patients required to be bled to faintness two or three times within thirty-six hours.'"

The stone communities grew, small tumbled Stonehenges of local mysteries. Who were the people whose names are growing as faint as starlight at dawn? Did they whisper stories to their children as they tucked them in? Were their voices rough as tree bark when they called their hunting dogs? Who did they love, and who loved them? And who will bring flowers and listen long enough in the silence to hear their old voices?

BARN RAISINGS

Sit in a barn, a big old bank barn, on a late summer's day, after the last bale of hay has been stacked and the sweet green scent rises around you. Dust motes hover and drift down the sun shafts that cut a swath through the dim interior, through doors thrown wide to welcome the swallows that nest in the rafters.

This much has not changed over the years, unless the farmer favors those round bales that hunker down in the fields like a herd of woolly mammoths.

Newer barns are sleeker, with fewer places to sit back and spin daydreams out of straw. If a barn has any age to it, the wooden floors have acquired a patina of smoothness from countless work boots crossing the wide boards, polished by hay bales sliding into place to form the base of those fragrant castles where kittens and kids play hide and seek.

The barn is a place of communion, a homely cathedral where man and animal share the blessings of the seasons. It is a shelter from storm, a setting for the dramas of birth and death. It is a place to think about the coming day and contemplate the fortunes of the weather as farmers parcel out corn and fork down hay.

The early barns in the county were hewn-log structures, built by the settlers' own hands with timber from their own lots. From the very beginning, by the old accounts, barns often served multiple functions, as public meeting halls and even as courthouses. Barn raisings were social occasions where the whiskey flowed as freely as the Rocky River at flood.

In June 1817, Rufus Ferris, land agent for Elijah Boardman, hired John Northrop and Nira B. Northrop to build the first frame barn in Medina. As documented in the 1948 *History of Medina County*:

> *The timbers being green and heavy, help was at that time necessarily obtained in part from Liverpool and Brunswick, and not being able to complete the raising in one day, all had to lie over until the morning. Ferris,*

Women served lunch to men at a barn raising. *Courtesy Medina County Historical Society.*

being fond of fun, prepared two large pails of milk punch, sweet, but strong with whiskey, and in a short time six or eight men were on their backs clawing around for something to take hold of!

This structure was the site of Medina's first term of court, the only building large enough for the gathering. At this time, Ferris "regaled the occupants of the barn with his favorite milk punch. The results were so disastrous…that Dr. Bela B. Clark, the only physician in the township, had to be called professionally."

The distribution of spirits crops up in one other barn-building account. John Coolman, who lived four miles southeast of Seville, used liquor as an incentive to entice neighbors to show up early for the long day of putting up a large double-log barn, although one might wonder what the pitch of the structure looked like when all was said and done.

Coolman invited settlers in Guilford, Westfield, Wadsworth and Milton Townships to the raising and "offered a gallon of whiskey to the locality whose representatives should be first on the ground." To ensure their victory, Henry Hosmer and the Guilford contingent left their homes at one o'clock in the morning, carrying torches to light the way, their axes slung over their shoulders.

Arriving at Coolman's about two o'clock, they woke him up, got the promised whiskey, took a drink all round and lay down by the fire to sleep till daylight. Just before daylight the Knupps arrived at the head of the Milton contingent and called on Coolman for the whiskey. They were much chagrined when he informed them that the Yankees [the Wayne County term for residents north of the county line] *had beaten them by several hours. Rather than disturb the harmony of the occasion, the victorious Yankees treated their rivals and themselves as well, to another drink all around before going to breakfast.*

A GLASS OF WHISKEY

As long as there have been those who never pass an opportunity to nip from the wineskin or tip the jug, there have been those equally determined to stop them. Read about any early construction project in the county and the account is almost sure to mention the pioneers' version of "Miller time." They not only raised high the roof beam but their tin cups of moonshine or homemade beer as well, which may explain why my dining room wall is a good three inches higher on the south side.

Authors of the 1881 *History of Medina County* explained it this way:

> *Like the early immigrants in all parts of the state, the first settlers of Medina County brought here the habits of intemperance which prevailed so generally in New England in the opening years of the nineteenth century. Whisky played an important part in all forms of social life in the new community. In the cabin, on training day, at loggings and house-raisings, at the meetings of the lodges and at ministerial gatherings, the lurking evil was found. Few distilleries were to be found in the county, but there was no lack of the product; drunkenness was common, and sudden deaths, of which whisky was the immediately producing cause, reach upward of a score in number.*

The county history book was quick to add: "But with this terrible vice, the people also brought an antidote, and it was not long before there were earnest men and women who united to combat the curse."

N.B. Northrop and Timothy Hudson were two early crusaders, and Litchfield Township hosted the first temperance society, formed July 4, 1832. Given the pioneers' preference for celebrating with gunpowder and firecrackers—and the short-fused tempers leading to another brand of fireworks—eschewing the hard stuff that day probably was a good idea, if any of those celebrating paid attention.

Other temperance groups may have formed earlier, and still others sprang up after. The Reverend W.B. Disbro edited the *Pledge*, a temperance paper, for the Medina Temperance Society in 1847. Sidetracked by the Civil War, it attempted a comeback in the early 1870s after "a few saloons were started in each of the principal villages in the county, and the druggists made the liquor traffic a prominent part of their business." (Including the sale of Lydia Pinkham's tonic to all those ladies for whatever ailed them.)

The revitalized crusade recruited the "best ladies in town" for visiting saloons and organizing reading rooms in their stead. County women jumped on the Women's Temperance League bandwagon on March 11, 1874, and the men followed with a league of their own in May. "The result was imminently successful everywhere. Saloons were closed, and druggists came upon temperance grounds."

The women's organization eventually became the Women's Christian Temperance Union, auxiliary to the state group. They created several groups for teenagers, the Young People's Christian Temperance Union and the Temperance Battalion, and one for children, the Temperance Gleaners.

A similar temperance phenomena, the "Murphy Movement," a secular operation founded by reformed alcoholic Francis Murphy, hit Medina in

1877. In response, a Young Men's Temperance Union issued "Murphy cards," on which the group's pledge was written. The cards were "popularly considered as a certificate of good moral character and a general passport to the favor of the people. There were numerous cases where these cards were secured and used for disreputable purposes, but in the main, the result was to advance the temperance sentiment."

Members wore a blue ribbon as their badge of honor, a practice later adopted by the Medina Christian Temperance Union. "Boys and girls of the village joined the 'blue ribbon brigade' and temperance meetings were held at the schoolhouse every afternoon at 4 o'clock."

WOMEN GET THE VOTE

On August 26, 1920, with the approval of the Nineteenth Amendment to the U.S. Constitution, women were granted the right to vote.

According to a September 1920 *Gazette* editorial, "The women in Medina County have never before been very strong in the slight opportunities heretofore offered them at the polls, neither have they been in the suffrage movements, but their interest so early in the Republican campaign shows that there is to be an awakening, at least so far as that party is concerned. More power to them."

Both Democratic and Republican Parties in the county made provisions "to take in" women voters. "Of greater interest and more importance than the mere opening of the [Republican] campaign, was the participation for the first time, of women in politics in this county. They responded to the call in splendid manner, and their presence and interest give assurance that they will be active in the campaign and with the party at the polls in November. It was certainly a good omen."

Dr. F.W. Boyer of Wadsworth, then vice-chairman of the Republican County Executive Committee, wrote a lengthy article urging county women to tackle this new responsibility.

> *The entrance of women into political activities, on a basis of equality with men on account of the ratification of the several states of the amendment to the Federal Constitution, conferring the right of suffrage on women, presents a new and interesting aspect in national politics.*
>
> *Personally, we are glad that we are living in the day that corrected this wrong to the womanhood of this republic...From this day forward, all the women of this country must take on the added duties of citizenship.*

Members of the Hammerschmidt, Borger, Longacre, Loomis and Burt families observe Armistice Day, November 11, 1918. *Courtesy Medina County Historical Society.*

He exhorted women to consider their party choices (the Republican choice in particular) and concluded with the admonition to women to be "politically wide-awake, perfect their organization and go to the polls early…and do their part" in securing a Republican administration.

Local women needed little urging. They embraced their new responsibilities and jumped right into the fray, selecting Mrs. S.F. Ross of Wadsworth as chair of the Republican Women's Advisory Committee. Mrs. C.E. Hoover of Medina served as vice-chairman, with Mrs. Jennie Bowman as secretary.

The women held an essay contest, in which participants had to explain why they were going to vote the Republican ticket. The top winner, Mrs. Vida D. Hostetler of Wadsworth, won ten dollars for her efforts: "I believe in the principles of Republicanism…that if Harding is elected he will surround himself with men who would be capable of dealing with Europe."

Democrats weren't sitting still, either, "and although they have not held many meetings so far, the time between now and election day will be well-crowded with speaking meetings. They are making much of the conversions of Frank W. Woods, E.R. Root and Mrs. A.L. Boyden and have induced each of them to make a speech."

The *Gazette* reported in October, "When it comes to real political enthusiasm, aggressiveness and push, hand it to the women of Lodi. The Republican women of that town held a meeting there last Friday evening and it was a crackerjack." Some two hundred of them were there, listening to three

Women turned out in force for the 1907 Memorial Day parade in Medina. *Courtesy Medina County Historical Society.*

candidates who made "rattling good speeches." And when a female speaker from Columbus failed to show up, Mrs. Jeannette Parsons of Lodi filled in.

That November, when Warren G. Harding took office, it was

> *a glorious victory, coming at the end of a campaign well-fought...And the women voted. From the long lines of them at the polls all day, it would seem that every woman was voting, but an analysis showed that only about 65 percent of them actually did vote compared with the men.*
>
> *The experience at the polls in Medina demonstrated that there must be another or two more election precincts, since at times it took over an hour to secure a ballot, there were so many in line. All succeeded finally in voting, who stuck to it, but quite a number left without doing so, declaring they would not risk their health standing out in the raw air.*

The first county woman to vote, Mrs. W.G. Frazier, cast an absentee ballot along with Mrs. Jane Partlon and Mrs. Tom Partlon.

Gazette reporters speculated the oldest woman to vote was Mrs. Cyrus Clark, checking in at 94. "Mrs. Sarah Winters of Lodi probably was next, having been 90 last April. Are there any older?"

Thirty-eight women served at the polls that day, including Hannah Clapp of Chatham Township; Mrs. Ina Cumberworth and Mrs. Edith Young of Granger Township; Miss Delsie Fulton of Guilford Township; Mrs. Nina

Horton, Mrs. C.B. Saunders, Mrs. Luella Griffin and Mrs. W.S. Brown of Lodi; and Miss Maude Hauck and Mrs. Robert Carr of Liverpool Township. Following the 1920 elections, a *Gazette* editorial summed it up:

> *Now that women have the ballot, and cast at the first election…there is no reason in the world why they should not be given a share of the offices. Here and there all over the nation there was a woman elected—a common pleas judge in Cuyahoga County, a clerk of courts in Wayne County, for instance— but in the future there is certain to be more of them. In two years there will be new officials at the Medina County court house, and the* Gazette *proposes right here that one or two or more of the vacant places-to-be will be filled with women. Any second the motion? All in favor say "Aye." Carried.*

MEDINA BURNED TWICE

Medina has twice mirrored the legendary phoenix, rising from the ashes of devastating fires that swept the square in 1848 and again in 1870.

The first spread rapidly from Barney Prentice's shoe store in the Mechanics Block to destroy structures around the square, including John Speer's printing office, the building housing the tinner's and tailor's shops, Chidester's Hotel and Dr. Munger's house and barn.

The *History of Medina County* recorded losses of $40,000 worth of property and noted that Judge Castle was able to save about $2,800 worth of goods, plus forty-six barrels of pork. Insurance covered some of the damages, but the Medina Mutual Fire Insurance Company at that time was nearly insolvent.

Although a hook and ladder company existed, many of its members "were not available, as the rules of organization were imperfect." When the alarm sounded in the early morning hours of April 15, 1870, firefighters still were not prepared to deal with a fire of such magnitude.

Many of the businesses had been rebuilt with bricks, but that did little to stop the flames that originated in an older frame building used as a barbershop just south of the square. (Later, two men arrested on suspicion of arson were released for lack of evidence against them.)

The roaring flames licked the sides of buildings in their path. They illuminated the town with a flickering, shifting light. Stars quivered in the dark as the intense heat shimmered upward. Sparks and burning cinders carried by the wind jumped to the Phoenix Block across the street, igniting Boult's dry goods store, McDowell's drugstore and Blake and Woodward's law office, with Phoenix Hall in the upper story.

Few trees graced Medina's square in 1868.
Courtesy Medina County Historical Society.

As a *Gazette* story indicated:

> *The town had no engine and in case of fire, the only reliance was the efforts of the people with buckets. There were ladders, and water was plenty in wells and cisterns. The population of the village turned out en masse and fought the fire inch by inch. They formed lines, men, women and children, taking their places in the ranks, and passed buckets of water continually, which was thrown on roofs, doors and windows. Wooden and tin pails, coal scuttles, wash pitchers, coffee pots, everything that would hold water, was brought into action.*

People dashed in and out of buildings, trying to salvage parts of their businesses, parts of their lives, before the fire reached them. They piled stacks of goods in the streets, only to have the flames take them in the end.

At 3:00 a.m., A.W. Horton mounted a horse and turned its head for Seville in hopes of recruiting their hand engine and a crew to man it. "As soon as he got there, and the news spread, the bells began ringing, and the people to the number of 60 or 70 started for Medina with the engine. When they arrived, the fire was in the Sanders building, and their efforts soon subdued it."

As people sifted through the charred remains, some odd mementos surfaced, like a ladies' gold watch belonging to Mrs. G.A.L. Boult, carried

Medina sustained heavy damage in the fires of 1848 and 1870. Firefighters were better equipped to handle the November 15, 1916 fire at the Independent Order of Odd Fellows Hall. *Courtesy Medina County Historical Society.*

by Ben Boult. "The night of the fire he left it in his vest pocket on his bed in the second story of the house on the Phoenix Block. It went down with the innards of the building and is in good shape to be preserved as a relic, but not of much use as a watch. It stopped at three o'clock."

When they hauled debris away, people determined to rebuild prepared the foundations for a new, better Medina. The history book recalls, "So far as adding to the beauty of the town, the great fire, like that of Chicago, was beneficial, inasmuch as it was the means of building it up with a much better class of buildings than generally found in a place the size of Medina...and are of a character any town may well be proud of."

A third fire of lesser impact in February 1877 burned the Empire Block and several adjacent buildings and motivated the purchase of a two-horse engine known as No. 4 Silsby Rotary Steam Fire Engine. Regular fire department personnel included E. Brenner, chief engineer; O.M. Jackson, first assistant; and Samuel Scott, second assistant.

TAKING THE COUNTY BY STORM

They called it a twister, a cyclone, "a huge demon of air...something diabolically grand...a fierce and irresistible elemental foe." But whatever name the newspapers tacked on the tornado, all that Medina County residents knew on Tuesday, April 8, 1890, was that the wind spiraled down out of a black sky and closed a tight fist around barns and houses and pulled them apart. It flattened trees and fences and uprooted dreams.

The county had enjoyed a good sugar spring, with warm days and freezing nights. In the February 13 issue of the *Medina County Record*, the Sharon Center correspondent wrote: "With the opening up of spring, and the bettering of the roads, the news begins to travel a little...Mr. Bettler has

People drove out to see damage from the cyclone that tore through Sharon Township on April 8, 1890. Several people died in the storm. *Courtesy Medina County Historical Society.*

A cyclone hit Medina Township on July 15, 1909, and killed a horse in William Richon's barn. *Courtesy John Gladden.*

the start of the sugar-makers, this year." But it must also have been a spring of storms, because a few days before the tornado touched down, "The high school gave a sugar-party last Thursday evening. The crowd was good, for such a night."

In that time frame, before Doppler radar and electronic weather prophets, when just about everyone hoed a large garden patch in addition to field crops, farmers listened to the earth and kept one eye on the sky before deciding when to plow and plant. Witnesses said the storm started "two miles south of Medina on the Seville pike…beginning its work during a heavy thunder shower."

Stories describing the storm are melodramatic in the literary and flourished style of the era, with one reporter summing up the event by saying, "All other news [is] crowded out by the cyclone."

The *Gazette* correspondent known as Graphite followed in the tornado's wake as it traveled across the countryside through Sharon Township, where it hit hardest. He described it as "a night's ride over muddy roads and under lowry skies amid anxious and excited groups of people."

The wind smashed a number of barns, including that of Christian Walls. "It is completely pulverized, and the strange part is the horses and cattle were unhurt. A big floor appears to have slid over them that furnished protection from the immense falling timbers."

Hail accompanied the high winds and damaged crops around the county. *Courtesy Medina County Historical Society.*

Heavy snows during the winter of 1914 contributed to floods in the county. This mountain of snow stood in front of Hobart's grocery store. *Courtesy Medina County Historical Society.*

Arthur Beach and Joshua Hartman lost fifty acres of maple forest. Fred Bettler would later collect a mountain of battered sap pails and evaporators salvaged from the downed trees. Worse, though, was the loss of life.

Rain poured down, and Sharon Center's fire bell summoned neighbors to help rescue trapped or injured families and their animals. T.S. Hammond, who lived south of the Hugh Frank farm, described the disaster that led to his neighbor's death. He was finishing afternoon chores in the barn and yard under a mass of dark clouds flecked with lightning.

"It was close and sultry and not a breath of air was stirring. I noticed that the cows and horses were unusually restless, but thought nothing of it until afterward. Presently the wind began to howl about the barn."

Hammond stepped outside in time to see the cyclone destroy Frank's house. Within minutes, Hammond, his son Chet and neighbors Xura Glingery and Aaron Thompson started out in the dark evening, carrying lanterns to search for Frank and his wife. The scene repeated itself in other pockets of the township as rescuers worked to free Mathew Bramley and N.L. Fulmer.

Most disasters attract crowds of bystanders, who mostly get in the way and hamper cleanup efforts, and this was no exception. By Sunday, strangers came to gawk "as long lines of carriages filled with sightseers rolled through the township." Residents largely ignored them, rolled up their sleeves and organized daily fence-building bees and relief for those who needed help.

People took refuge in a wagon to survey the floodwaters in Seville. *Courtesy Medina County*

Floodwaters rolled past McCabe's restaurant in the village of Seville. A group of diners peered out the window. *Courtesy Medina County Historical Society.*

Summer crept in, muddy roads toughened under the sun and barns blossomed again over the ruins. The survivors coped with their losses, wept together, made the storm a memory that lay just beneath the surface of the spring and then got on with the business of everyday things. The next year, the farmers went out again to the maples with buckets and spiles and waited for the thin sweet music to complete the circle.

KIDWAGONS AND LITTLE RED SCHOOLHOUSES

Before there were backpacks for books, there were satchels equipped with handles or a long strap to sling over one shoulder. Or you clutched your books and papers against your chest as you scuffed through the leaves on your way to and from school, all the while dreaming of Friday afternoon and freedom. If you didn't walk, you rode the bus, a practice that seems pretty tame compared to what pioneer children contended with.

Elmira Loomis, born in Harrisville Township in 1817, grew up to be Mrs. Amasa Parsons. She often told stories of watching the family flock of sheep to keep the wolves away. On her way to school, Elmira sometimes caught sight of a bear.

Instead of buses, students rode horse-drawn kidwagons to early classrooms, and a lucky few saddled their ponies and headed for school.

In Homer Township, the first school was built in the Williams District. It was a log hut with log seats and a murky interior, with the only light coming from the open door and "an aperture in the wall," according to the county history book written in 1948.

Samuel Vanderhoof donated land for a second school, Elm Tree Hall, a mile and a half east of Homerville. "The men who hewed the timber for the building were paid $1.25 a day for 'self and cattle.' Miss Lucretia Young was the first teacher in this district."

Five more schools followed, including Frog Pond School; Woodville University, commonly known as the Eyman or Kemery School; and the Barone District School. By 1906, a centralized school was established, with 175 pupils enrolled—Homer was the first township in the county to have complete centralization. Teachers were Superintendent L.M. Newcomer, Rose Harbaugh, L.V. Jeffery and Vella Eberly.

There was a "little red schoolhouse" in each corner of Spencer Township, plus one south and one north of town.

> *These one-room schools with their uncomfortable benches, wood stoves and poor light would seem very inadequate to us now. One can see very plainly the old box stove with pipe running the entire length of the room. The children near the stove would roast, while those at the outside would shiver with cold. The old water bucket with a dirty tin cup stood in the corner, and the pupils would ask days in advance for the privilege of passing or carrying water up and down the aisle.*

The school year ran six months. Female teachers, employed for the three-month summer term, earned twenty dollars per month, while men received thirty dollars per month for teaching the winter term.

Spencer schools produced such notables as John Stone, who served in Congress with Blaine, McKinley and Sherman and later became chief justice of the state of Michigan; Common Pleas Judge George W. Lewis; and Dr. James Freeman.

Students and teachers form a circle on the front lawn of the early elementary school in Medina Village. *Courtesy Medina County Historical Society.*

Children attended the centralized school in Granger Township. *Courtesy Medina County Historical Society.*

Sharon Township schoolchildren pose for the camera. *Courtesy Sharon Township Heritage Society.*

The Mennonite College served students in Wadsworth. *Courtesy Medina County Historical Society.*

NORTH BY NIGHT:
MEDINA'S UNDERGROUND RAILROAD

While the master slept in the big house, the slave family hushed the dogs with meat scraps they had carefully saved and slipped away from the cabin beyond the cotton fields. Father, mother and two children, they ran through the cicadas' song to the shallow river, where their footprints melted like sugar and washed downstream.

Traveling north by night toward Ohio, they followed the map of their hearts and the star shining in the handle of a drinking gourd in the sky. The North Star hung above the pines like a Christmas candle burning a hole right through the dark that they wrapped around themselves like a cloak.

Clutching their forged passes, the family looked for signs marking the stations of the Underground Railroad. They shivered, even though it was July, and the corn whispered around them like old men rocking on a porch telling secrets.

They moved from station to station, walking on their own or hidden in wagons under straw, sometimes allowing themselves to lie in coffins for safe transport.

Above Ripley, running to Columbus, they threaded the northern towns on the strings of their memories and made a necklace of Redoak, Fincaste, Sinking Spring and Sugar Tree Ridge.

In Medina County, they could add Hinckley, Medina, Westfield and Granger Townships to their map of safe spots. Among the antislavery men who provided shelter and meals for runaways, the most prominent were Harrison G. Blake, John McCloud, Halsey Hulburt and Hiram Miller. They risked imprisonment and fines up to $1,000.

McCloud, who lived in Granger, and Miller, a Hinckley resident, were outspoken activists in temperance as well as in the abolitionist movement. When the church to which McCloud originally belonged opposed free thought, he founded his own "Church of Liberty" and served as its leader. The strong-spirited McCloud, whose abolitionist views may have been shaped in part by his own cruel treatment as an indentured servant when he was nine, assisted runaways for more than thirty years. Liberty Hill, located on his property on Remsen Road just east of State Road, became a focal point for his railroad operations.

According to the 1881 county history, Miller "deemed it his religious duty to use his best efforts in aiding runaway slaves to escape…Some residents in his neighborhood were hostile to his movements of humanity, and often sought to discover slaves in his care, in hopes of getting the promised reward; but no runaway who sought his protection was ever captured."

Miller appeared undaunted by threats. It is possible that he helped almost one thousand people escape, feeding and hiding them until he secreted them either under straw or in wooden freight boxes in a wagon and carted them to Dover Bay, west of Cleveland.

The station keepers' families were at risk as well, and whenever Blake had railroad visitors, his two daughters stayed home from school, just in case they were tempted to reveal the secret.

Blake hid the runaways in the attic of his home on the southeast corner of Jefferson and Washington Streets, or in the barn at the back of the property,

People mourned the passing of H.G. Blake in 1876 by hanging crepe on the Phoenix Bank building. Blake, a prominent businessman in the county, was also a conductor on the Underground Railroad. *Courtesy Medina County Historical Society.*

before taking them to Oberlin. He remained a "conductor" from 1830 until he enlisted in the Union army in 1861.

Hulburt, who lived in Westfield Township at the corner of Hulburt and Seville Roads, served as a township trustee for several years and later as director of the Ohio Farmer's Insurance Company.

INTERURBAN TO MEDINA

Say "trolley" and people think of San Francisco, but trolleys of the Southwestern interurban system once ran through Medina, carrying milk, mail and passengers to points south and north of the village. On sultry summer days, people packed picnic baskets and boarded the train for an afternoon at Chippewa Lake. Party groups chartered trolleys that became known as "opera cars" so they would have a way home from Cleveland after performances, because theatres let out after the last train ran.

The heyday of the electric railway in northern Ohio spanned the years between the appearance of the Cleveland & Berea Line in 1883 to the demise of the Cleveland Southwestern Railway & Light in 1931. At its height, the Southwestern, known as the Green Line, had 215 miles of mainline track.

Norman Muller worked in Southwestern's substation maintenance division. In a 1994 interview, the interurbans still traveled the lines of his stories. He flipped through worn pages of albums thick with photographs—the cars, the motormen, the conductors, the places they traveled. The names made their own music when he spoke about Nickelplate Crossing, the Rockport Yard and Cottlesbrook Switch.

Men from the Medina Creamery Company get ready to board a special car reserved for them on the Cleveland Southwestern Railway and Light interurban system. *Courtesy Medina County Historical Society.*

"The first rail cars of the Cleveland-Berea line were battery-powered, but sometimes they ran out of juice before they reached the end of the line, and a team of horses had to finish the job and pulled them to Rockport or Berea," Muller said.

He tapped a picture of a car named "Alvesta." "This was a prime car on the Cleveland to Columbus run, named after the wife of the president of the Southwestern line. When he sold his stock in the company, they renamed it 'The Mansfield.'"

Long before Muller worked the line, he rode the interurbans and recalls one morning in particular when he took a streetcar to Sunday school. After he boarded, he realized he couldn't find the nickel his mother had given him for the fare.

"The conductor, Arthur Beebe, kept telling me if I couldn't find it, he was going to put me off." The nickel never turned up, and Beebe did put the youngster off, but not until they reached Muller's regular stop on Fifth Street.

"There was a milk stand at every crossroads, where the farmers brought their milk cans. A shoe-shine rag and polish were kept under the stands, so you could shine your shoes while you waited for the cars to come."

The electric railway came as far as Medina in 1894, but as late as 1899 county officials and townsfolk dithered about granting a franchise through Medina to extend the line to Chippewa Lake and Seville.

A letter to the *Gazette* editor favored the venture and a route taking the line down Court Street to the American House Hotel, west on Liberty to Hinman's corner, south on Prospect to Smith Road going west past the fairgrounds. The corner of Court and Liberty was "practically the center of population of Medina and gives all a convenient access to the business portion of the village, and that a stranger passing through…sees the best part of the business as well as some of the finest portion of the residence part of it, and so forms a much better opinion of us."

The line eventually did extend to Chippewa Lake and on to Seville, where it split. One section branched off to Wooster, the other threaded its way through LeRoy, Lodi and West Salem on its way to the end of the line at Bucyrus.

According to a *Gazette* item published May 29, 1903: "On and after May 30, Cleveland and Southwestern traction cars on the southern division will leave Public Square, Cleveland, hourly fifteen minutes after the even hour, for Berea, Medina, Chippewa Lake, Seville and Creston, and run through without a change of cars."

A round trip to Chip cost fifteen cents, and sometimes the transport proved less than reliable. A July 8, 1904 account reported, "The broken down electric car service kept many at the Lake long after they meant to be home, and some from Cleveland did not get home till the next morning."

Medina's semipro baseball team eventually became part of the Northern Ohio Trolley League, named because the players rode to games via trolleys.

Businessmen took "circle trips" on the interurban, riding the Alvesta parlor car to points on the line and stopping to tour the towns. The first from Medina, made by a ninety-member contingent, left at 7:00 a.m. on October 3, 1911, and visited Creston, Seville, LeRoy, West Salem, Ashland (where they dined on fried chicken at the Hotel Otter) and Mansfield before looping back home.

Not all of Muller's memories were gentle ones. "The Dolores" served as the line's funeral car. Painted lavender, it could accommodate two caskets. Family members sat in the front half of the car, with friends in the back half. During the World War I influenza epidemic, Muller said the car made two or three runs a day. Many cemeteries had a siding for the funeral cars, he said.

Accidents and derailments were not uncommon.

Muller described No. 111 as a hard-luck car. "A little girl was killed on the tracks, and later, the 111 killed two men on a motorcycle. They pulled in front of the car in Lorain."

A Southwestern car struck and killed Seville resident Newton Clapper as his wagon crossed the line at Main Street in Seville.

Wrecks on the interurban lines running between Cuyahoga and Medina Counties were not uncommon occurrences. *Courtesy Medina County Historical Society.*

"It is supposed," the *Gazette* account reported, "that he did not think of the crossing, seeing the other wagon go over ahead of him, and the rattle of the wagon is supposed to have drowned the noise of the approaching limited from the north."

The advent of the auto diminished the electric railway, and buses took over much of the passenger transport. Muller recalled how the last train rolled into the barns in Cleveland.

"On the last day, a lot of the employees' wives rode with them, the last day their pass would be good," Muller said. "Harold Hull was the motorman on the last run through to Cleveland, January 31, 1931, on the southern division. I was in the barns when Buss Karshner, the motorman, brought in the last one on the western division, Feb. 28, 1931, the Lorain-Elyria run. He blew four blasts on the horn. That was it."

"CENTRAL, HOW MAY I PLACE YOUR CALL?"

In January 1900, the *Gazette* chronicled the struggle with new technology—the telephone—and how it became a prankster's tool.

> *"Hello there, Ganyard, someone wants you here at my new telephone." County surveyor Ganyard, in his unmistakably earnest way, came in from his real estate platting in the commissioners' room to answer the call Recorder Hart announced was waiting for him on the new phone in his office. Before the surveyor picks up the receiver, be it noted that no connection had been made and no wires run into this phone: It looked like any other phone, but yet it wasn't.*
>
> *"Don't know much about this telephone business, but I'll try it on," said the surveyor. "What shall I do first?"*

He was instructed to say hello and then ring until he got an answer. Ganyard dutifully began, alternately ringing and speaking. He continued about five minutes, not noticing when Hart excused himself to the next room, so he could "hold his sides (presumably to contain his laughter) and lean up against the wall as he listened to Ganyard: 'Hello! Hello! Hello! Durn ye, hello, I say! Can't ye hear nothing? Dangfound ye, hello I say!' To save the surveyor's mental soundness, ex-surveyor Sheldon came to the rescue and told Ganyard to wait until the phone was connected…Now Ganyard looks at Hart with a look of unconcealed suspicion."

It used to be you opened your window and leaned out to talk to your city neighbors if the houses were close enough. Farm families came into town for market day with words saved up to spend and trade, too. You talked at the feed store, the dry goods store, Grange meetings, socials, after church, at Ladies Aid or sewing circles and when visiting.

It was big news in 1882 when the *Gazette* announced that Cleveland and Akron soon would be "telephonically connected." And once upon a time, a crank call meant something entirely different than it does today. To place a call during the first half of the century, you lifted the earpiece to make sure the party line was clear (or to listen in on a bit of gossip), jiggled the cradle, cranked a handle on the side of the phone box and waited until a crisp voice on the other end said, "Central, how may I place your call?" Party lines were a source of community information, a sort of local news wire service.

Today's long-distance carrier wars are mild in comparison to *Gazette* headlines of March 7, 1901, that summed up a telephone war of that era as "Outrageous!"

> *There is a new kind of telephone war in Medina—hot, ugly and with at least two lawsuits in sight. This local uprising—for it is the indignant citizenship of Medina against the vandalism of a telephone company— was occasioned by some night work of the Western Reserve Construction gang now stringing the U.S. Telephone Co. wires in this town. These men (or someone doing their work) after midnight Monday, went with a team*

Early switchboard operators placed calls for the customers. At one time, seven phone companies served Medina County. *Courtesy Medina County Historical Society.*

to L.S. Smith's and J.T. Ainsworth's residences, slashed and marred two handsome shade trees, doing it in the roughest way, gathered up the debris and stole away in the darkness of early morning.

This occurred after Smith had gone to F.H. Leach, president of the Medina Telephone Company, to protest any unauthorized tree cutting. Leach countered that Barr, the foreman, had been instructed not to touch any trees "until proper leave was secured."

In a confrontation with Barr at the American House Hotel, Smith said the foreman sneered and said, "You just go on and find out who did it. I've seen wise fellows in country towns like you before."

The village council brought charges against U.S. Telephone, Medina Telephone and Western Reserve Construction and its foreman, but the parties settled out of court. The U.S. Telephone Company had to apply for its own franchise and pay all costs in the suits against the workmen and "reasonable damages" for the trees, determined to be about $100.

THE MAIL WENT THROUGH

In the "good old days," houses rarely had heat upstairs, and on frigid mornings, children huddled around the kitchen stove as they dressed. People traveled by wagon or sleigh, with heated bricks to warm their feet and heavy blankets across their laps. If the temperature dipped below zero, like it did for a long stretch in February 1899, people either stayed home or added another brick.

The *Gazette* reported frostbitten ears, toes and noses but "no serious freezing of anyone." Vegetables froze in root cellars, the ice on Chippewa Lake thickened to a foot deep and several feet of steam pipe froze at the Medina Methodist Church, yielding a "plumber's bill and no church Sunday evening."

Wild weather nearly stopped the postal service, despite its promise to deliver through snow, rain, heat or gloom of night.

Mail carrier William McKay, who was "Celtic, of good courage and employed by A.H. Thomas to drive his mail team," left the Medina Post Office at 10:00 a.m. in a two-horse buggy with three "tie-sacks" of newspapers and one pouch of letters. When he

reached Rocky River at the covered bridge, he looked eastward to the farther shore across a raging main. Gathered neighbors warned William not to

U.S. Postal Service carrier on Rural Farm Delivery Route No. 5 in Medina Township gets ready to roll. *Courtesy Medina County Historical Society.*

Mail carriers line up outside the Seville Post Office. *Courtesy Medina County Historical Society.*

attempt the crossing. But lofty determination sat upon William's brow and scorn curled his lip.

"I'm hired to carry this mail, and I'm goin' to carry it o'er; and if I don't they'll find me dead upon yon farther, wave-swept shore."

Well, maybe in his Celtic soul he said that, and maybe the reporter added a touch of poetry, but at any rate, McKay urged his team forward. He didn't go far.

Something caused William to reflect; then to pause; then to stick his feet upon the dashboard out of the water; then to grab to the mail sacks…the water was up to the horses' backs and running swift…Certain destruction was ahead; an amused crowd of spectators behind and no woods for William to take to. So he took to the water to try to unhitch the team.

McKay was having a really bad day; as he struggled against the current, his employer stood on shore and urged him to hurry.

"William got his head above the roaring main and with a little breath of two parts air and three parts water, replied: 'Goldarn ye, if you want 'em unhitched in such a dogged-on hurry, come in yourself.'"

Needless to say, Thomas didn't move.

When McKay finally succeeded and the horses swam to safety, he grabbed the buggy as it "went yachting down the swift current till all brought up against a tree." Neighbors threw him a rope and hauled him to safety, "William sometimes submerging and sometimes on the crest."

He managed to retain the pouch of letters, and "the buggy and the three tie-sacks of papers were secured after the flood Sunday morning."

The headline of this little gem, "In the wild flood," first caught my eye, but the subhead was what really intrigued me: "Mail carrier McKay did his duty to the U.S. but got soused."

"Soused" is sometimes a colloquial term for "drunk," and given the historical accounts of how much whiskey men imbibed at barn raisings and public celebrations in the county, I didn't think it was too unusual for someone to resort to spirits for fortification to get the mail across a raging river. After reading the story, I'm wondering if "soused" actually should have been "doused," and maybe it was the typesetters who had a bottle close at hand.

HARVEST OF ICE

On hot July days, the iceman took massive ice tongs and hauled a big block of winter's harvest to the wooden icebox in the kitchen. The kids looked forward to those days, when the iceman handed them dripping chunks of ice to suck on as a treat since there weren't ready-made cubes or Popsicles on hand. One might argue that ice has no fragrance, but ask anyone who has held winter to their lips on a sweltering afternoon about that cool sweetness rising around their face.

At the turn of the century, Chippewa Lake provided a prime source of ice for the county. When December turned the corner into the new year, it was not unusual for the *Gazette*'s Chippewa correspondent to report on the weather as it applied to taking ice from the lake.

On January 18, 1889, the conditions were "no nearer winter yet; the prospect for a supply of ice next summer begins to look more dubious and the idea of sleigh riding this year has gone glimmering." When February gusted in, the "thermometer marked about zero Wednesday morning… Good winter weather at last."

A few days later,

> *Ice on the ponds is from four to six inches thick. Now is the time to harvest it. It may get thinner instead of thicker by waiting. Some was taken out of Huntington's Monday about five inches thick.*
>
> *The ice crop that is now being gathered in this vicinity will fully satisfy all expectations, and there will be no ice famine this coming summer. All the local ice houses have been filled, and work at Chippewa Lake, where the Knickerbocker Ice Co. of Cleveland is filling several large houses with a choice lot of ice, is progressing nicely.*
>
> *About a hundred hands with a number of teams are at work, and ice is being put up at a rate of three or four thousand tons a day. A new ice house has recently been erected by the company which is 300 feet in length, 62 feet wide and 40 feet high, and will hold about 25,000 tons of ice. It is now nearly filled.*

When the Cleveland, Lorain and Wheeling Railroad built tracks that carried passenger cars to the lake, a line of track was extended to the icehouses. Once the cakes of ice, which measured about a foot thick and were "two feet square," were loaded on the train, they traveled as far as Philadelphia, Pennsylvania.

Teams of horses plowed the frozen lake surface clean and scored the ice for cutting, which was accomplished with saws. The horses were fitted with spiked shoes so they wouldn't slip. Drivers tied strong ropes on the animals in addition to the regular harness so the horses could be pulled out if they fell into the frigid water.

Workers cut a channel that would be kept clear so they could float the ice blocks toward the icehouse loading area to conveyer belts that ran inside the structure. They stacked the blocks and shoveled sawdust around them to keep them from freezing together and to minimize melting.

In 1889, the cold weather held until March 15. "The ice harvest closed at Chippewa Lake last Tuesday evening. The last of the ice cakes were hauled up in boats to the inclined plane chutes. Work continued for about twenty days, and from 30 to 40 tons of ice has been cut up, and all of it fine quality. Chippewa Lake, not alone being the greatest pleasure resort of the state, is today also the leading ice field of Ohio."

Later articles indicated that lightning struck and destroyed the Knickerbocker Company icehouse on July 4, 1902. Other companies that cut a profit from the lake included Minglewood Ice Company in Wooster and the Forest City Ice Company.

PART II

PASTIMES AND PLEASURES: SHOTGUNS AND APPLE PIE

Chippewa Lake, Lafayette Township

Before the first settlers cut roads into the Western Reserve, before the hunting parties of Iroquois and Delaware and other Native Americans followed deer through the forests, the land and the lake of Lafayette Township belonged to those wild mysteries of wind, earth and sky.

They belonged to the fishing heron and the fox, the wolves running like silent gray ghosts though the mist and the otters slipping in and out of the lake.

Pioneers forced the Indians to other lands, claimed the territory and named it for the Marquis de Lafayette. Frame houses followed log cabins, wild trillium and daisies gave way to wheat fields and men harvested ice from the lake.

"In coming years," wrote the authors of the 1881 county history book, "the approaches to the lake will be improved, larger and better places of resort will be erected on its shore, pleasure vessels of various kinds will be launched upon its waters, the sedges and grasses growing so luxuriantly along its borders will be removed and possibly replaced…with stone and gravel, thus providing a beach for those desiring to bathe, and the village will be frequented by pleasure seekers from home and abroad."

The writers proved to be fair prophets. About 1870, Edward Andrews, who lived on what was known as the Upper Grounds of the lake, created a pleasure resort around a restaurant and dance hall. He added "a roller coaster and merry-go-round, provided a pier and had boats for rental. Swings hung from the tall forest trees, and picnic tables were added."

Several years later, with the addition of a hotel and cottages, Chippewa Lake became a focal point for picnics and excursions.

Lakeside cottages and hotel rooms offered city dwellers a change of pace at Chippewa Lake. *Courtesy Medina County Historical Society.*

Wading in the water and picnicking proved popular pastimes at Chippewa Lake. *Courtesy John Gladden.*

A brass band furnished music during the season, and…every child saved his money to buy some of Andrew Nelson's "ice cream candy" either vanilla or strawberry flavor and wrapped in tissue paper…and part of the pleasure in getting the candy was watching the expert swinging the huge mass of taffy over a large iron hook that was fastened to a tree or post, and pulling it out to be slung over the hook again until it was just the right consistency to cut into slabs of candy about 5 inches long and 2 inches wide, and sold at two sticks for a nickel.

The lake continued to be a popular summer spot, particularly for the annual "Business Men's Picnic." Despite the title, it was a family day, with baseball games, concerts provided by the Knights of Pythias band, dancing during the afternoon and evening, water races and a number of contests we'd probably consider unusual today.

In 1910, John Mayberry beat Glen Kindig in the boys-over-twelve barrel-walking contest, while Charlie Adams, Rufus Kennedy and Marion Dague

Families and businessmen enjoyed carefree days at the lake. *Courtesy Medina County Historical Society.*

Mineral springs were just one of the attractions at the lakeside resort. *Courtesy Medina County Historical Society.*

The giant oak dwarfs Terry Tavern at Chippewa Lake. *Courtesy John Gladden.*

trailed Fred Koons, winner of the fifty-yard running-backward race. The boys also had a piggyback running race, carrying a partner for one hundred yards, a tub race and a raft race.

Women and girls got to compete in foot racing, ball throwing and knot tying, a contest judged by how many different kinds you could tie. Mrs. E. Woodruff tied the most, followed by Mrs. W. Kindig, Mrs. A.J. Waltz and Mrs. H. Adams.

Dwight Walker beat Max Phillips, Fred Hoyt and Howard Calvert in the eat-three-and-whistle free-for-all cracker-eating contest; the D.R. Peltons won the largest family award; and D.S. Longacre had the dubious honor of winning the three-jumps-backward-for-fat-men contest.

THE BOYS OF SUMMER

It is late in the school day, and the hands of the clock have slowed to a snail-stuck-in-molasses crawl. They couldn't possibly move any slower, because it is April, it is baseball weather and will the final bell never ring? The warm, brisk breeze has rattled the classroom windows all day, teasing the boys who must instead cipher and struggle with neat penmanship and the proper way to parse a sentence. It is spring, and who cares about the ancient Greeks when there are baseball dreams sliding into home plate? Unless Homer wrote a baseball odyssey, they don't want to hear it.

They want to talk, live, eat, sleep and dream baseball. The boys lollygag on their way to school in the morning, listening to the old men speculating on the local teams as they sit on benches, warming their bones in the sunshine. In the spring of 1905, it is all about the new C&SW Trolley League. The *Gazette* writers wonder if the town will support the kind of team needed to face "such strong nines as Wooster, Elyria, Norwalk and Lorain have organized...But the company will be faster than last year, and a regular league organization formed, with provisions made for salaried umpires, forfeited games, etc." Eventually it boiled down to four teams—Medina, Wooster, Norwalk and Elyria—and Medina had to cough up about $400 for a guarantee fund.

The boys brag, smacking their fists into their gloves, nonchalantly tossing the battered ball into the air and catching it. They could be the Medina County Stars, they say, looking sadly at the sunshine as the school doors close behind them.

The Stars played their first game against Elyria on June 7 at the fairground diamond, defeating them eight to four. The Stars were a mix of homegrown talent plus five from Cleveland added to the roster. The Cleveland contingent consisted of Tellinde, who "isn't pretty, but he's the goods in baseball," as pitcher; Segrist White, "a lightning third baseman and good swatter," described as one of the best all-amateur hitters; shortstop Gebhardt; and Cushing, a "sure catcher and dead shot throwing to second."

Praise for the local team members was a little backhanded in the *Gazette*:

> *Chatfield, though out of practice, played a fine game at second... "Old Tom Case" (may the dews of Heaven ever fall gently on him, for we love him still) collided with the ball in his own terrific style for three bases—and it would have been a home run easily, had not Thomas Case's legs given out at third. This great strike for victory drove in two runs. Freddie Taylor of Seville made one of the prettiest bunt hits ever seen on the grounds, while General Bounds got in one good swat. The home guards did their full duty.*

Little boys weren't the only ones enamored of the game. Baseball dominated picnics, reunions and other social gatherings, spurring would-be athletes to possibly unwise contests. The *Gazette* published a flurry of insulting challenges from the Litchfield Leans, the Seville Fats and the Solid Men of Medina.

One, from the Fats to the Leans, published July 21, 1905, went something like this:

> *Ho, you skinny, umpire-buying, dude-rigged, bony sons of emaciation, who call yourselves Knights of the Imperial Order of Leans. Be it known to you by these present that the Gentlemen of Weight refuse to acknowledge defeat in last Monday's game, justice and truth being submerged under your clandestine and wicked pre-arrangement with the umpire; therefore, we dare and challenge you to put on your dude clothes again next Wednesday, bring on your martial band, bats and conceit, and meet us in fair and honorable baseball warfare...July 26 at Chippewa Lake....Now, you umpire-fixing, skinny common disturbers, do you dare?*

W.C. Smith, captain of the Leans, replied: "You bet we do. Get your old hulks of fat out of the hospital and be ready. We will be there.—P.S. We expected nothing less than that frizzled fat would calf, and blame it on the best umpire ever seen here."

The paper delighted in reporting these games, no holds barred with its coverage, as noted in the July 21, 1905 description of one skirmish between Fats and Leans. The Fats, led by Ben Wells "gowned in a bathrobe," donned white caps and shirts, short blue jeans and red stockings, with their weights marked on the uniforms. The Leans wore white everything—duck trousers, shoes, stockings, collars, neckties and caps.

The Fats boarded a hay wagon on the square, with Ganyard's martial band leading the way to the fairgrounds. The Leans rode in cars, chauffeured by A.I. Root, S.J. Swain and A.L. Boyden. The one-hundred-degree temperature didn't discourage the eight hundred fans who turned out to encourage their favorites.

The Leans' strategy, to let the Fats take a huge lead and wear themselves out,

> *worked to perfection. At the end of three innings, the score stood 11 to 4 in favor of the Fats, who then began flying distress signals in every quarter. Ab. Oatman's pitching arm melted off. Geo. Boult's old legs gave out, as did Wells' and Schlabach's mouths—a sign of awful exhaustion. Doc Wise was wind-sucking like a bellows after two fearful trips around the bases. Alvin Robinson alone showed any signs of life or hope. After the third inning, they were too far gone to even talk. Then the noble Leans quit playing possum, Lewis Randall replaced Mayor Van Epp in the box, and the slaughter of the groaning, melting dying old Fatties began. The Leans piled up 15 runs in the next three innings, the final score being 19 to 14 in favor of the Leans.*

In statistics below the story, the needling went on, with digs like: "Handsomest men on the grounds—the 9 Leans; Ladies choice—the 9 Leans; Struck out of their class—the Fats; Meanest talker on the sidelines—N.P. Nichols."

Meanwhile, back in the Trolley League, the Medina Stars continued a break-even season, eventually winning thirteen and losing twelve to pull themselves into third place. They had a final moment of glory in the 1905 season when they defeated the Elyria champions in the last game. The team retrieved some shreds of dignity, coming back after a whopping sixteen-to-three loss to Elyria the previous week.

"The team has been playing the fastest kind of ball during the past six weeks, devouring opposing teams with a vim that would have landed Medina in first place this year if the spirit could have been exhibited earlier in the season…to take the final game from Elyria by a score of 4 to 2."

EATING CROW: THE SPRING HUNT

At the turn of the century, a group of Medina County men gave new meaning to the term "eating crow" when the success of their crow-hunting exploits ended in buying dinner for the winning team. It was a familiar theme reported annually in the *Gazette*, particularly since publisher H.G. Rowe was one of the key players. His team went head-to-head with Ben Wells.

One of the highlights of the year for county hunters was the annual crow hunt. *Courtesy Medina County Historical Society.*

There was no history of the competition, but I suspect it may have started as a boast over beers in the local tavern—one of those "I'll bet I can spit farther than you can" taunts made from the bottom of a glass.

In the March 28, 1901 *Gazette*, they laid the ground rules:

> *To each and every hunter we say get every crow and hawk you can by means of a shotgun April 5, but not before that day nor by means of money or friendship. Forget the past and be crow honest...Dr. W.D. Wise will act as judge on the time of death of each crow presented for the count and his decision will be final. He knows the difference between a black hen and a crow, and knows a crow that has been in cold storage.*

Wells, anticipating a good hunt, rose early—the first shot fired at 3:00 a.m.—but the early bird got only one crow. His neighbor and opponent, "awakened by Ben's early antics, arose, went forth in humility of spirit and afoot, but came back at dewy eve with six crows."

By the time the April 11 edition went to press, it was all over.

> *At 7:30 in the evening the Brenner House had all the appearance of receiving election returns. The place was packed. Every returning warrior was greeted with a cheer or a jeer. Dr. W.D. Wise was on hand to examine every crow. Benjamin's killings were first counted and numbered 30. Rowe's warriors had deposited their killings in a huge black pile that was found to contain 42. The doctor-judge declared in several cases on either side the date of death was very uncertain, but counted none out. When the result was announced, cheer on cheer rang through the hotel, and there were glistening tears in both of Ben's sad eyes.*

As the evening wore on, a few men questioned the integrity of some hunters after they trotted out the "preservation of game" subject. The toastmaster called on Wise, who said, "After seeing W.B. Chapman's and Court Sears' crows, he thought they could tell more about the preserving business than anyone else. Chapman responded by saying the best way to preserve crows was to keep them out of Ben Wells' reach," a comment which in turn led to a discussion of conscience in crow hunting.

"Dr. John Weber responded…by saying he had left his speech on a stump in Mallet Creek. As for conscience in a crow hunt, it was like snakes in Ireland—there are none. After a man waited for hours under a brush pile and never gotten a crow, conscience would not prevent his using any means to get one."

J.W. Seymour, a Medina attorney and one of the "Wells gang," looked thoughtful throughout the discussion of conscience, although he was preoccupied not with moral philosophy but personal economics. The hunt cost him dearly, he said, and enumerated his debts: "Telephones to Liverpool, 85 cents; cartridges, 45 cents; livery, 55 cents; six boys hunting all day at 50 cents each; this supper, 75 cents. 'I brought home two crows and I didn't shoot either of them.'"

THE LADIES AID OF REMSEN CHURCH

When Hazel Stoll, a member of Remsen Christian Church, set out in 1982 to write about the church's Ladies Aid Society for the group's ninetieth anniversary, she wanted to get beyond dates and events. She delved into the secretary's book, recorded in 1892. The book itself enchanted her—small and brown, with "Compositions" printed across the top, the cover pictured a mother walking down the path from her cabin to meet her young son coming home from school. The elegant lines of calligraphic script recorded their dreams for the church.

Like all Ladies Aid societies, the group raised money for its church through cooking and serving community suppers, and it seemed prophetic that the members held their first meeting on Thanksgiving Eve 1892, one day after the church officially organized. Mrs. Height, the storekeeper's wife, hosted them at her home near the church. Thirty-three members paid ten cents for annual dues.

To raise $144 for furniture and carpeting for the new church, ten cents became the magic number—the price of a home-cooked meal. The women held dinners at noon during the winter and served suppers in the late summer afternoons.

They set down strict serving rules. At dinner, they served only "one kind of meat, two kinds of vegetables, bread or biscuits, one kind of pickle, tea and coffee, pie or pudding." Supper fare included "bread or biscuits, one kind of sauce, cold meat or cheese, one kind of pickle, pie or cake and tea." You faced a fifty-cent fine if you were caught filling a friend's plate with both cheese and meat.

The women devoted one autumn meeting to "canning enough grape juice to take care of Communion for the next 52 Sundays," the heady scent of fruit clinging to them as they stepped out into the early October sunshine.

When they weren't cooking, they quilted, charging seventy-five cents per spool of thread, twenty-five cents to tie comforters. Sometimes the sound of ripping cloth set the rhythm of their meetings as they tore carpet rags for one cent per pound. With a vote of eight to three, they selected Washington's flag as their first group quilt pattern, finishing in time to raffle it off at the "indigo and ice cream social" held in the Grand Army of the Republic hall.

James Reynolds, of Weymouth, bought the quilt for $3.00 in a bidding war with Lura Crooks—a profit of $1.50 after materials. But the women always came back to the food, serving noodles and biscuits, ice cream, cake and cookies before the young people—and some not so young—played "Snap, Catchem and Kissum" and bingo.

By the time they cooked and sewed their way through a summer ice cream and strawberry festival and a Christmas bazaar, they exceeded their goal by forty-four dollars. To celebrate the dedication of the new church building October 29, 1893, they whipped up a free meal for the community.

What Stoll saw in the record books, between the lines, was a community of women working together. Although the day might have worn cool blue skies trimmed with gold leaves, the kitchen would have been hot. The women wiped their hands on towels and aprons and pulled pans of chicken and biscuits out of the oven. They peeled apples to slice, sugar and tenderly tuck under a pie crust to be lightly browned. As the kitchen grew even hotter, the women pushed damp wisps of hair away from their pink cheeks with the back of their hands.

Steam trailed behind them like the tail of a comet as they carried out heaping plates of meat and wedges of pie still warm. The small music of cups and plates bumping each other in the dishpans filled the room, the clatter of silverware like a drumroll. Maybe someone started singing, softly at first, then louder, as they washed and stacked plates, as they stepped out and walked home under the stars burning into the dark above the church bell tower.

The bandwagon provided a mobile bandstand for concerts on the square. *Courtesy Medina County Historical Society.*

THE MUSIC MAKERS

All stand and hats off! Members of Medina's prospective new band met with the Knights of Pythias committee in the town hall last evening. Sixteen or 18 players are already in sight, and the instruments are to be ordered at once.

Three cheers for the band boys and Medina's new band! A better day is coming in the near by and by!

While Medina didn't exactly have seventy-six trombones parading around the square, the 1899 *Gazette* article makes it sound like the "Music Man" paid a visit—and he must have made a few other stops throughout the county at one time or another, judging by the formation of a number of community bands that were the forerunners of today's groups.

Several years later, the Medina band performed at a Knights Templar conclave in Louisville, Kentucky.

Perhaps 500 were at the depot to see them off, and the strains of "My Old Kentucky Home," played as they marched, excited curiosity enough in a town that seldom hears other open-air music than church bells on Sunday.

The Medina Band is right in it with two of the best bands in the United States. Three Commanderies from Washington, D.C., are attending... Washington Commandery No. 1 is accompanied by Haley's Band... that furnished the music for the last inaugural ball. With Columbia Commandery No. 2 is the full U.S. Marine Band of 45 pieces under Santelmann himself.

The Knights of Pythias Band entertained crowds around the county and once performed in Washington, D.C. *Courtesy Medina County Historical Society.*

The 1899 band was not the first in Medina's history. Blake's Hall provided the setting for the March 8, 1860 presentation of a banner (at a cost of forty-eight dollars) to the Medina Cornet Band.

"C.J. Warner came into the hall carrying the banner, followed by Miss Georgia Beatty, wearing a black silk dress with white scarf." The rest of the ladies' delegation—Miss Cornelia Babcock, Julia Turner, Esther Alcott, Hattie Loring, Matilda Hayslip, Hattie Chidester, Maryette Butler and Helen Nickerson—each wore a blue scarf. Band members included Philo Chase, H.P. Welton, J.T. Ainsworth, B.F. Parmeter and Mark Ferris.

The group must have prospered, because they received $725 worth of instruments in 1865, and in 1872 the *Gazette* reported, "The Medina Silver Cornet Band is in fine shape and the band wagon is to be repainted and slicked up." One year later, band members sported new uniform coats, black with white buttons and silver epaulets.

The Granger Sax Horn Band appeared even earlier, with notice of a concert performed by the Barron family in March 1858, and Seville musicians got in the act in 1907.

Orchestras also flourished and performed at various local dance halls and functions. A 1906 teachers' institute at the Phoenix Hall featured Seville's Euterpean orchestra, assisted by soloists Paul Chase and Miss Martha Miller. The latter also served as the group's pianist, with cornetist Eddy J. Miller, Dr. H.E. Hard playing clarinet and Charles Rogers on violin.

The orchestra apparently derived its name from Greek mythology's Euterpe, the muse of music and lyric poetry, and performed admirably.

The Seville Band put on a good show in 1907. *Courtesy Medina County Historical Society.*

"Not withstanding the extreme heat, the hall was nearly filled, and the audience showed by their hearty applause how well they were pleased with the entertainment…All were…compelled to respond to encores."

Hartman's Orchestra furnished some swinging tunes for a dance hall that Frank Chidsey and Thomas J. Huffman opened May 13, 1916, in Weymouth. "Messrs. Chidsey and Huffman announce that good order will be insisted on at this new dancing resort at all times and that no rowdyism of any sort will be tolerated." The orchestra stall dominated the middle of the east wall of the building, which boasted a maple dance floor, plaster walls, a decorated metal ceiling and a gasoline lighting plant providing illumination.

The fifty-piece Medina Symphony Orchestra had its moment of fame when it performed a concert broadcast nationwide from the Cleveland Plain Dealer studio, WTAM, on October 29, 1923.

S.H. Brainard, secretary of the Medina Kiwanis Club, engineered the opportunity for the concert and notified more than 1,200 clubs throughout the United States, urging their members to tune in. Kiwanis members furnished the musicians' transportation to Cleveland and threw a dinner party at the Hollenden for them.

Ruth King, who screened entertainers before they were allowed to perform for the station, "expressed amazement that a town the size of Medina had produced so wonderful an orchestra as the one she had just listened to."

For those who didn't own radios, "a receiving apparatus will be stationed in the auditorium of the high school building and operated by R.E. Snedden. A nominal admission of 10 cents will be exacted, all the proceeds from which will be turned over to the high school athletic fund."

PART III

MEDINA COUNTY CHARACTERS: ROGUES AND POETS

THE LAST CIVIL WAR SOLDIER

There is one Civil War soldier left in the county. Flanked by two long, sleek Parrott cannons, he is stone and cast metal and stands sentry atop the memorial erected "to the soldiers of Medina County, 1861–1865." His only enemy now is the weather, and, like a tired child, his gaze is fixed on some distant dream, some place where all the fighting ends and home is just over the next hill.

Medina County sent hundreds of men to fight in what President Abraham Lincoln referred to as a "fiery trial" in an 1862 message to Congress.

Frank Derr, a Sharon Center native born in 1847, chronicled his reaction to the conflict:

> *One spring day when I was thirteen, father and I were working near the woods when Silas Chandler…came over to tell us that war had been declared between the North and South. I shall never forget the peculiar feeling that came over me at the thought of war. Four young men on adjoining farms enlisted and fifteen enlisted within a radius of two miles. The war songs were a great feature and were sung with great spirit, intensity and solemnity. Whenever a group of young people came together, these songs would be sung. All would start out bravely, then one by one they would falter and stop with perhaps one-half of them in tears. Nearly every one of them had a dear friend or relative in the army.*

Peter P. Cherry, who edited a local paper called the *Young Folks' Gem*, wrote: "The war governor of Ohio telegraphed each county in the state—'Citizen

The Civil War monument at Spring Grove Cemetery stands watch, flanked by two Parrott cannons. *Courtesy Medina County Historical Society.*

soldiers of Ohio wanted to defend Cincinnati. Terms of service, one month or more. Must furnish their own arms and ammunition. Haste is desired. They shall be called Squirrel Hunters of Ohio and upon discharge shall receive certificates to that effect.'"

Joe DeNardi of Granger Township, a retired elementary school principal with a passion for history in general and the Ohio regiments of the Civil War in particular, commented on the attitudes of the soldiers. "People were different then," he said. "The men would stand and fight against incredible odds and then simply say, 'I did my duty.' Most people today would have been out of there."

Some reasons for enlisting then were not so different, though, considering a portion of a letter written by H. Wolcott, who stated: "I am deprived of all the conveniences of life...Father says if he was a young man, he would go...Most every boy has gone to the army...We haven't got any harness, buggy, saddle not one horse fit for use."

A later letter sent home showed a Wolcott matured by his service: "We have been back from our Morgan hunt just long enough to get our company together once more...You wanted to know if I could get a furlough to go home. I do not think that I can, and even if I could, I do not want to go home until I get through soldiering."

DeNardi pulled out one thick volume after another, searching for information as he talked. "One Sharon Center boy, Brookens H. Brittain, died in Andersonville Prison, in Georgia, August 4, 1864. He was a member of the 125th Ohio Yankee Tigers."

He paused reflectively. "That was a good regiment. They had hardly anyone left at the end of the war. The Eighth Ohio formed in Summit County, but it had a lot of Medina men in it. Their skirmishers (men sent out ahead of the regular line) are credited with contributing to the failure of Pickett's Charge. They didn't retreat when they should have and a large number of Confederates stopped to fight," he explained.

DeNardi said the regiment repelled three major attacks, and in the end 102 men were either killed or wounded. Officers were elected for each company. In the Eighth Ohio, Captain Ora O. Kelsea and First Lieutenant Philo Chase led Company H, while Captain Wilbur F. Pierce, First Lieutenant Henry W. Fritz and Second Lieutenant Otis Shaw Jr. led Company K. They were all from Medina County.

CHARLIE OLCOTT: A POET'S SOUL

November holds the solemn days of souls and saints.

Charlie Olcott, drawn to Medina County in 1818 when thick forest still surrounded the settlements, was no saint, not by a long shot, but he had a poet's soul. It is true he was given to writing rather sentimental love poems during his middle years, but perhaps it was the ability to merge the mathematical precision of meter and rhyme with words that also gave him the means to visualize the possibility of ironclad ships that would float by more than faith.

In his heart of hearts he was an inventor, the kind of man who believed he could hold moonlight in his hands and not be branded by its quicksilver coldness.

But moonlight has a way of marking those with the kind of softly mad vision Olcott possessed. Born in 1793 in Manchester, Connecticut, a Yale scholar who could read Greek and Hebrew, he preferred to dream of ironclads. He may have doodled designs on the edges of the notes he took while he studied law, letting them sail the distance of imaginary seas while he walked from class to class.

When the powers that be told him his ideas were as insubstantial as dandelion fluff, he didn't abandon them entirely. He buried them only deeply enough to finish school and practice law, becoming Medina's county prosecutor from 1826 to 1837.

Described in a *Gazette* story as a pudgy man with "florid face and untidy appearance" and a "vagabond in his habits of life," Olcott cared more about his inventions than the conventions of proper dress and cleanliness. Perhaps because he was often "filthy to an unspeakable degree," he was an attorney without clients, although he also served as Medina's justice of the peace in the 1840s.

He kept an office in the old courthouse, where Whitey's Army-Navy store stands today, sleeping on a small cot in one corner, surrounded by ship models crowding every available surface, some hanging from the ceiling. In 1848, he wrote a letter to a Yale classmate:

> *My whole life, with few exceptions, has been spent in the most resolute and persevering efforts at moral, political and scientific reforms and I have shared the fate of all original...reformers that have preceded me, namely poverty, reproach and unceasing persecution. My iron-ship invention which I made in the summer of 1815...will finally be adopted for all ocean navigation.*

An avid abolitionist, he frequently contributed long letters on the subject to the *Gazette*. He also wrote a three-hundred-page treatise, combing through pages of scripture and historical texts for proof that Jesus was an abolitionist, too. And, of course, there were the poems.

When George Redway reminisced in the July 9, 1909 issue of the *Gazette*, he quoted Mrs. Bostwick, who knew Olcott when she was a child. He had written poems about unrequited love and romance in her mother's album, using red ink and careful flourishes, but he also explored darker subjects such as mankind's future destruction:

> *Volcanoes smoke with fearful sound*
> *And shake the solid earth around*
> *And cities bury underground*
> *In ruin there confined;*
> *And subterraneous fires below*
> *With never-ceasing fury glow,*
> *But fiercest fires their rage bestow*
> *Upon the immortal mind.*

Olcott suffered a stroke and spent his final days at the county infirmary. Bostwick, who lived in New York, wrote to Redway: "Poor old wise simpleton! I called on him while he was an inmate of the Medina County infirmary where he was made very comfortable. He was a patient listener to the complaints of other inmates and mourned because he could only give them words of sympathy and no tangible relief. I think the old cemetery in Medina was his burial place."

THE GIANTS OF SEVILLE: CAPTAIN BATES AND ANNA SWAN BATES

When we take the measure of a man, it is usually depth of character to which we refer. But in the late 1800s, when Captain Martin Van Buren Bates and his wife, Anna Swan Bates, moved to Seville, it was probably difficult not to talk about measure in terms of skyscrapers or sequoias. Better known to many simply as the giants of Seville, they towered over their neighbors, sunflowers in a field of daisies. Local legends, their story has endured for more than a century.

Anna stood a regal seven feet eleven and a half inches tall, a good two inches taller than her husband, although he was vain enough, in writing his own booklet about their lives, to claim he equaled her in height.

Captain Martin Van Buren Bates and his wife Anna Swan Bates pose in formal dress. *Courtesy Seville Area Historical Society.*

Born in Nova Scotia in 1848, Anna began working for showman P.T. Barnum when she was sixteen and later for Judge H.P. Ingalls. She met the captain in 1870, when he agreed to tour Europe as a member of Ingalls's company. I don't know if it was love at first sight for them, but they married shortly after their arrival in England. Anna, clad in white satin and orange blossoms, sporting a cluster diamond ring given to her by Queen Victoria, wed the captain in the ancient Church of St. Martin-in-the-Fields. They toured halls and castles and dined with dukes and kings. Talk about fairy tales.

To imagine giants as neighbors was a foreign concept to many people, yet that's how many people in Seville regarded them after the captain purchased a farm in Guilford Township as a place to settle down.

"I think when they retired, they really wanted very much to put their touring days behind them and become part of the community," said Fay Wanko during her term as president of the Seville Historical Society. "People at that time were cordial with them. He [the captain] had some nastiness, but they dealt with it."

After retiring from show business, Captain Bates and his wife made their home in Seville. *Courtesy Seville Area Historical Society.*

The captain's autobiography testifies to his yearning for success. "I had determined to become a farmer, so I stocked my farm with the best breeds of cattle, most of them being full-blooded shorthorns," he wrote. "My draught horses are of the Norman breed. Carriage horses eighteen hands high with a couple of Clydesdale mares constitute my home outfit."

"If you'll pardon the pun, they wanted to keep a low profile," said Don Gottlieb, curator of the Seville Historical Society Museum. "They did take an active role in the community. We have photos of him at a G.A.R. reunion and at the Masonic Lodge. It must have been difficult for him as a veteran of the Confederacy. We had our own [Union] regiment from here, so it would have been hard for the community, too."

Trying to blend in would be difficult in any case. The couple built an immense house furnished with sofas and chairs that left guests' feet dangling inches from the floor. The captain's Clydesdales pulled a carriage designed to accommodate their tall frames, and a special pew at the Baptist church ensured a comfortable place from which to worship, but despite that, they were, like Goldilocks, in a world where nothing was "just right" for them.

While many of the stories handed down explain how they coped, others testify to the captain's quick temper—and humor. Like the time he overheard men in the village store loudly discussing Bates's strength, a scene described by Lee Cavin in his book *There Were Giants in the Earth*, published first in 1959. The proprietor remarked that "if that so-called strong man can lift one of those barrels of sugar like I just had to, he can have it!" The captain hoisted the barrel, which Cavin estimated weighed more than two hundred pounds, and walked to his home more than a mile away. He returned to the now-quiet store and asked, "Have you got any more sugar you want to give away?"

The giants had a soft side when it came to children. Cavin wrote about Mabel Mapledorm, who remembered sitting on the captain's lap during services at First Baptist Church. If she fussed, the captain soothed her by holding his large, gold pocket watch—the same one given to him by Queen Victoria—to her ear, much like putting a ticking clock in with a whimpering puppy.

"He hid penny candy in his coat pockets," Gottlieb said. "He may have had a soft spot for kids since they lost two of their own." Anna gave birth to a stillborn daughter when the couple lived in London, and an infant son, the largest baby on record, died shortly after birth.

"The kids [that visit the museum] are always surprised at the size of the cradle," Gottlieb said. "But mostly it's the size of the giants themselves and the fact they lived here that amazes them."

The giants continue to cast a long shadow, their cutouts on display at the John Smart House Museum in Medina. Did they mind the notoriety, the sometimes not-so-surreptitious stares when they walked into church or drove their outsize buggy down the road?

We can only guess at the private castles they built in the clouds. Unlike Jack, we have no beanstalk to shimmy up to get a glimpse. We have only the old accounts to go by, like the one cited by Cavin and written by the captain in which the latter concludes: "With this exception (their son's death), our lot has been one of almost uninterrupted joy. To you and our friends we wish equal pleasure, and may peace and happiness dwell with the reader."

CIVIL WAR SAMPLER

It is said that at the Battle of Chickamauga the bullets flew so thick and fast they cut down trees. Whether or not that is a truth stretched, it takes only a small step of the mind to imagine what it did to the men on both sides.

In a display case at the county historical society, visitors can see a bullet embedded in a fragment of white pine from Chickamauga, flanked by a square of perforated tin the soldiers used to grind field corn into meal, artifacts of life and death, side by side.

Men and boys enlisted in what they thought would be a short war—sign up in April, be home by Christmas and the other side would be whupped good and proper. Some of the soldiers fulfilled their ninety-day obligations and went back to their fields, stores and offices. Those who reenlisted after their initial tour of duty spent three years chewing on hardtack biscuits so tough they earned the nickname "sheet-iron crackers" and dodging disease as well as bullets.

Ohio men were so eager to enlist when President Abraham Lincoln called for soldiers that the state's troop quota was met and surpassed within two weeks of the call-up. Numerous Medina County men answered the summons, among them Theodore Wolbach of Wadsworth; Lorenzo Vanderhoef and his two brothers Orange and Orson of Homer Township; and six Nichols brothers, Harrison, Henry, John, Charles, Albert and Daniel, of Sharon Township.

Charles Nichols died from wounds received on the skirmish lines and illness claimed John, but the remaining brothers returned home. Both Wolbach and Vanderhoef kept extensive diaries of their experiences.

Vanderhoef's writings were published by the Patten Free Library in Bath, Maine, in 1990, under the title taken from his first entry, *I Am Now a Soldier!*

His Civil War story begins with his enlistment on April 27, 1861, when he and several companions from Medina joined what became Company K of the Eighth Ohio Volunteer Infantry.

As the war progressed, Vanderhoef's entries mirrored the man who started out with having "a jolly time going up to Brighton" on the way to Camp Taylor for training and ended as a war-toughened soldier wounded and left for dead in Bloody Lane at Antietam.

Training was inadequate, camp conditions were largely unsanitary and food was miserable and often scarce once troops left the main encampments. A typical day passed with hours of drill, learning bugle and drum signals, and bayonet practice that often resulted in wounds more severe than those received on the battlefields.

Soldiers passed the evenings with impromptu baseball games, foot races, singing, whittling (one source indicated they even bowled tenpins using cannonballs) and reading and writing letters.

All of Vanderhoef's diaries survived, with the exception of the volume leading up to and including Antietam. He cherished letters from friends and family and wrote back with detailed accounts of Company K's experiences. The journals reflect the transformation from a great and glorious adventure to a grim ordeal. Vanderhoef learned loneliness and wrote of homesickness, visualizing his family going about their daily tasks before he readied himself for the next march, the next bloody battle.

Despite the horrors the soldiers saw and experienced—or because they faced them together—veterans created the Grand Army of the Republic in 1866. Members, who pledged to keep alive the memory of those who fought to preserve the United States, campaigned for the rights and pensions of veterans and/or their surviving families. They banded into regional posts and met on a regular basis.

Vanderhoef, forced to give up farming due to his war disabilities, eventually entered government service at the Treasury Department's Bureau of Statistics in Washington, D.C., where he joined the GAR Burnside Post No. 8.

Wolbach often mentions GAR meetings in his postwar diary entries: "I had a call from Comrade Waffle pertaining to county relief for Mrs. Jane Brown, widow of a Civil War soldier." His entries even list members who attended.

The GAR spawned the Sons of Union Veterans of the Civil War on November 12, 1881, still an active national group today. Reenactments weren't uncommon, either, judging by an 1883 *Gazette* announcement of a two-day grand encampment and basket picnic at Chippewa Lake.

"Old veterans will fall into line with their regiments, as all soldiers are invited to participate. The Bummers [nickname of General Sherman's troops in Georgia] will be present. The great amusement attraction will be the 'Hillsdale Spy'…one hundred mounted men, seven hundred infantry and several cannon will do the realistic battle, and natural scenery will be used."

The Memorial Day issues of the *Gazette* honored surviving Civil War veterans, chronicled their passing and exhorted readers to "keep green the graves and memories of our country's brave…Strew flowers here—fresh, radiant flowers! With beauteous buds and blossoms rare, cover the silent mounds. Wreathe the white tablets o'er with fragrant garlands. Here sleep the brave."

JIM BROWN, GENTLEMAN ROGUE

He strode through town with an easy grace, hat pulled rakishly low over one eye. Tall enough to look men square in the eye as he firmly gripped their hand in greeting and gracious enough to doff his hat in a sweeping bow when introduced to ladies, the description in old news accounts describes Jim Brown as "a gentleman rogue of first water, of fine personal appearance, large, tall and handsome, of good manners and fine address and liked by everyone who he hadn't done out of money."

Although indicted by a Medina County grand jury March 8, 1839, for counterfeiting and later found guilty and sentenced to seven years in the Ohio penitentiary, townspeople did like the man:

> *Brown's word was as good as gold. No one ever doubted it. While held under heavy bond, he was allowed the freedom of the town by the Sheriff, to whom he gave his word that he would report at every meal time and at bedtime. S.H. Bradley and J.H. Albro can relate how he used to visit their stores at this time and was the best-liked man who came in to "loaf." He was a gentleman and a gallant to the ladies and a favorite with the men.*

Brown was reputed to be the leader of a gang of horse thieves and counterfeiters operating throughout northern Ohio. They camped in log shacks in the Yellow Creek Basin on the Cuyahoga River and used an old tavern near the northern Ohio depot in Medina as a rendezvous point.

> *One of his strong plays in deviltry was to prove an alibi. There were no railroads, and to do this he made rides on horseback that seemed incredible…*

in the night and after having played some bold hand in his haunts in Summit County he would turn up conspicuously in Cleveland, Toledo, Youngstown or Pittsburgh so shortly after the commission of his crime elsewhere that no jury would convict him, believing it impossible for him to be where the crime was committed and so far removed a few hours later.

His most famous ride took him from Summit County to Toledo in one night.

Like a pony express rider, Brown used a relay system, with his accomplices waiting at key points with fresh horses so he could leap "from one horse to the other only to continue his thunderbolt ride to the westward." Imagine a ride through the countryside in the moonlight—I'm thinking there had to have been a full moon to cut a path for him through the darkness as he rode toward the morning side of midnight. And everyone seems a tad crazier during a full moon.

People at the little crossroad settlements would have muttered in their sleep, turning over and pulling the blankets up around their ears as Brown guided his horse past their dreams. Or did he slow his mount to a walk, the only sounds the soft creak of leather as he shifted in the saddle, the soft jingle of bridle chains as the horse snorted and tossed his mane, his coat dark and slick with sweat in the starlight?

Men may have envied Brown for his wild ways, and ladies perhaps hoped he'd raise their hand to his lips for a chaste kiss.

At any rate, there seem to have been few or no complaints when Brown's lawyer, Squire Floyd, "secured papers from a higher court in Cleveland" and overturned Judge Dean's sentence, preventing Brown's incarceration at the penitentiary. The sheriff released him a few days later, "the case against him being nolle prossed by county prosecutor Israel Camp."

IDA EDDY, NO ORDINARY WOMAN

When Mrs. Dayton (Ida) Eddy presented her speech at the January 1900 edition of the Poe and York Farmers' Institute, she sounded like a woman ahead of her time, judging by its title: "The Farmer's Wife: Some Things for Husbands To Remember and Wives Not To Do."

Although she opened with scripture describing the creation of woman as man's helpmeet, she quickly added: "The divinely ordered plan seems to be that man shall find in woman a helper, a partner, not a little dog to run hither and yon at his call, nor yet a pretty toy to be kept in the parlor for his amusement." Eddy defined helpmeet as "a coworker with him; one who

Lucy Adelia Washburn looks out the window of her airy kitchen. *Courtesy Medina County Historical Society.*

The Washburn women could personify the words of Ida Dayton Eddy in her speech to the Farmer's Institute. *Courtesy Medina County Historical Society.*

shall stand by him in the battles of life; one who shall give love, sympathy and often counsel; one whose fine instinct shall sometimes serve him better than his own stern judgment."

Eddy asked why some women chose to become "anything but a farmer's wife" and forwarded the theory that the true definition of helpmeet got lost

> *in the mechanical performance of necessary duties…Poor woman—she flies from one thing to another until her brain is all in a whirl; she works from early morn till late at night with scarcely a moment to rest; she must get three full meals every day, because there are hired men; she must be amiable when the man of the house sends in for the hammer, and she has to take her hands from the bread dough to go and find it; she must not lose her temper even though she has to bring in her own wood, chase the pigs from the front dooryard about 57 times a day and go to the barn for the fragment pail which the men forgot to bring back after emptying.*

The man of the house, Eddy insisted, should be expected to help make the woman's work easier:

> *Don't compel her to parboil herself in a little stuffy kitchen…Let her have a large, airy kitchen on the sunny side of the house with pantry and cellar handy. Don't make it necessary for her to go down a flight of steps every time she goes outdoors. Don't make her go to the neighbors for every pail of water she uses, or dig some potatoes before she can cook them for dinner.*

Don't come in, Eddy wrote, and whine at your wives about the neighbor who calls her men in at half-past eleven and then ask why she can't do the same. Eddy's words conveyed the picture of a no-nonsense kind of woman who tied on her apron with the same sense of purpose a general has when he marshals his troops for battle, and woe to the man who questioned her worth. She would be small and wiry, with strong arms from churning butter and rolling out miles of pie dough. Her fingers would be tough enough to strip a cow's udder and tender enough to tuck a wisp of wayward hair back into her daughter's braids.

If her husband came in and asked about why she couldn't match her neighbor's lunch schedule, he might be wearing his soup promptly at eleven-thirty. Shrewd in her observations, she was quick to suggest the male half of the marriage team had better do his part, particularly in money matters.

> *If you think you need a new corn planter or cultivator you do not hesitate to buy it; let her have the same privilege in her domain. Don't always wait*

till she asks you for money, and don't deal it out grudgingly. Just because it is paid into your pocketbook instead of hers is no sign she has not as perfect a right to use it as you have.

But let me not be too severe on the "lords of creation." Many of them are without reproach in these respects and are as thoughtful and considerate as mortals can be expected to be.

Eddy commended women who kept a neat, orderly house, but admonished them not to achieve it at the expense of their health. Her philosophy was to let them eat cake, but only once in a while. There were things more important than extravagant dining.

"Peace of mind and sweetness of disposition in a household are worth more than cake and pie and pickles, and the temper of the housewife often gives the keynote to the whole family. Housekeepers are sometimes credited with being too cross to live with, when in reality they are too weary to put one foot before the other."

Given a choice to bake a cake or take a ride with her husband, Eddy's preference was clear.

"It will do you good to get away from the cookbook for a little time. It will rest you to look at the fields and woods as you ride and you will forget that you have to work hard. It will do your husband good to have you go with him. If you do not, he may forget to ask you the next time he has a similar errand."

But Eddy also encouraged women not to succumb to self-pity over hard times. "If you are where God meant you should be, then be happy and contented and make the most of your opportunities."

RUSSELL ALGER, SECRETARY OF WAR

The days are shorter and softer now, leaning toward November as the leaves drift earthward. Wildflowers begin to wither along the roads, leaving them looking tired and barren—with the exception of the crop of campaign signs that spring up faster than mushrooms in the rain.

Debates begin and the hot air and heated words rise, cooled only by the reality of returns and final tallies. Many politicians begin with good intentions, but sometimes they get snarled in party lines or tripped up by congressional pigheadedness.

Such may have been the case for Russell Alger—born February 27, 1836, to Russell and Caroline Alger in Lafayette Township—who served as President William McKinley's secretary of war. He fell into ill favor during the Spanish-American War, when more U.S. troops died from disease than in battle. Alger was blamed for not having appropriate medical preparations.

Lafayette Township resident Rhonda Jones believed Alger got a raw deal. "Everything I've read indicates he began to investigate the condition of the services after McKinley appointed him," she said. "He felt the number of surgeons, nurses and supplies was inadequate and went to Congress with a request for more. They told him no, because at that point they didn't believe there would be another war." That left Alger as McKinley's whipping boy as troop losses rose, Jones said, adding that people called him "the murderer of youth." He resigned.

Jones said more recent evidence seemed to indicate that McKinley planned to go to war with Spain but hadn't shared the information with Congress. "Today Alger would have held a press conference and backed up his innocence with the numbers he showed Congress before the war."

She believes McKinley felt responsible for Alger's predicament and discreetly appointed him to congressional office in 1902 to fill the seat of a deceased senator. Alger was reelected to the position, which he served until his death in 1907.

"There are a lot of loose ends to follow. You start with one and it leads to another." Jones became interested in Alger's struggles when she started to research the history of her house, built in 1837. What she discovered was the Alger family, who once owned a large parcel of land in the township.

Russell Alger was thirteen when his parents died within months of each other. Two uncles, David Alger and John Alger, shared custody until Russell went to live with his grandfather in Richfield, then still part of Medina County.

By 1859, Alger, described by Jones as tall and lanky, with a long, Abraham Lincoln–like face, practiced law in Cleveland. "He was a colonel in the Union army and in 1864 was 'brevetted a major-general,'" Jones said, quoting a history text. "After the war, he moved to Michigan to take advantage of the building boom there. He made millions in the lumber industry. The Alger family is still prominent there today—there's a county named after him."

Politics beckoned, and Alger served as governor of Michigan from 1885 to 1887 and national commander of the Grand Army of the Republic. A favorite son for candidacy in the U.S. presidential primary, Alger ultimately lost his bid for office.

"But he was held in high esteem by the party, and he was a friend of McKinley's who appointed him secretary of war." Despite Alger's political misfortunes, Jones believes he should be remembered more for selecting Teddy Roosevelt as commander of the Rough Riders.

"U.S. history would have taken a different turn had Roosevelt not been pushed into the limelight."

A.I. Root, Friend of the Wright Brothers, Entrepreneur

Amos Ives Root leaned closer to the gold chain he worked on in his jewelry shop on the square. He liked sitting near the window, watching people pass by as he designed tableware or bracelets. Sunlight flooded the room as he brought his creations from rough sketch to finished product. When a shadow fell across his hands, he frowned and looked up.

A swarm of bees clustered on the window, obscuring the view.

"What will you give me if I can catch those for you?" one of the workmen asked him as they listened to the bees hum against the glass.

"I'll give you a dollar, one day's wage," Root said, not believing for an instant he could do it.

The workman snatched up a box and loped out the door. It wasn't long after that he reappeared with the bees bumbling inside the box. "You catch the queen, the others follow," he told Root, quickly pocketing the silver dollar.

Root carried his new investment home, where his wife questioned the sanity of his purchase.

The Wright brothers invited A.I. Root to watch some of their early flights near Dayton, Ohio. *Courtesy Medina County Historical Society.*

"What good are they?" she asked.

Over the course of the next few months, Root found the answer. He ferreted out all the information he could find about bees, driving his horse and buggy to Cleveland to conduct research. His one-dollar prize eventually led him to sell the jewelry shop, build larger quarters on West Liberty Street and embark on a new career. He improved a hive design developed by the Reverend Dr. Lorenzo Langstroth and sold hives, smokers and other beekeeping equipment in addition to marketing honey. The publication of circulars in response to other beekeepers' requests for information planted the seed for *Gleanings in Bee Culture* magazine and a book, *The ABC and XYZ of Bee Culture.*

He incorporated windmill power in his plant, no surprise to those who knew his penchant for gadgets and inventions.

John Root, A.I. Root's great-grandson, who related the stories, said his great-grandfather became a close friend of the Wright brothers, winning their trust enough to earn an invitation to one of their test flights near Dayton, Ohio.

"He was interested in what they were doing," Root said, adding that the letters A.I. wrote to the Wrights have been published on the Library of

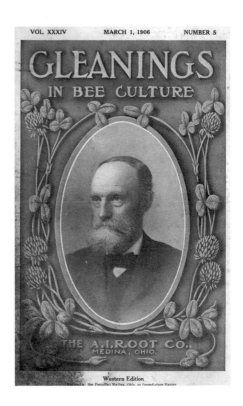

A.I. Root wrote, edited and printed *Gleanings in Bee Culture* magazine. *Courtesy Medina County Historical Society.*

Congress website. "He knew it [flight] was going to be important to our future. He wrote letters to convince them [of his sincerity and interest in their work] to allow him to come and watch. He included a penny postcard for their response."

At least seven letters later, Amos Ives Root watched history in the making at Huffman Prairie, a meadow seven miles east of Dayton. He wrote about it and the initial flights in *Gleanings in Bee Culture* magazine:

> *You and I have in years past found enjoyment and health in sliding downhill on the snow; but these boys went off to that sandy waste on the Atlantic coast to slide down hill too; but instead of sliding on snow and ice they slid on air. With a gliding machine made of sticks and cloth they learned to glide and soar from the top of the hill to the bottom; and by making not only hundreds but more than a thousand experiments, they became so proficient in guiding these gliding machines that they could sail like a bird and control its movements up and down as well as sidewise. Now, this was not altogether for fun or boys' play.*
>
> *It was my privilege, on the 20th day of September, 1904, to see the first successful trip on an air-ship, without a balloon to sustain it, that the world has ever made, that is, to turn the corners and come back to the starting point. During all these experiments they have kept so near to soft marshy ground that a fall would be no serious accident, either to the machine or its occupant. In fact, so carefully have they managed, that, during these years of experimenting, nothing has happened to do any serious damage to the machine nor to give the boys more than what might be called a severe scratch. I think great praise is due them along this very line.*
>
> *When Columbus discovered America he did not know what the outcome would be, and no one at that time knew; and I doubt if the wildest enthusiast caught a glimpse of what really did come from his discovery. In a like manner, these two brothers have probably not even a faint glimpse of what their discovery is going to bring to the children of men. No one living can give a guess of what is coming along this line, much better than anyone living could conjecture the final outcome of Columbus' experiment when he pushed off through trackless waters. Possibly we may be able to fly over the North Pole, even if we should not succeed in tacking the "stars and stripes" to its uppermost end.*

The same curiosity that drew him to flight led him to his own adventures with a velocipede, an early version of the bicycle. He read about velocipedes in *Scientific American*, and "as soon as I saw the description, I sent an order for

Root raised queen bees at the company apiary. *Courtesy John Gladden.*

one, and I think I had about the first machine in the semblance of a bicycle that was ever in Ohio." He paid $100 for it—much more, he said, with shipping prices tacked on. "When it came to hand, after days and weeks of anxious waiting, neither myself nor anybody else could ride it at all. The whole town jeered at me, and the story of the 'fool and his money' was hurled in my teeth so many times I almost dread to hear it even yet."

Maybe his wife would have called it stubbornness, but Root was nothing if not persistent. He spent hours practicing and rented a large hall where he could practice in private. Once he mastered turning corners and made a complete circuit of the room, he took his show on the road around the square.

"He was interested in a lot of things," John Root said, adding that his great-grandfather received a four-page letter from Helen Keller after he offered to help her foundation dedicated to educating blind and deaf children.

Throughout the remainder of Root's life, beekeeping remained the heart of his business, which employed about eighty people and grew to include a tin shop, carpenter shop, blacksmith, machine shops, printing office and book bindery. Almost three acres of apiaries housed 228 hives dedicated to rearing queen bees. Root's honey products later earned Medina the nickname of the "Sweetest Town on Earth."

PART IV

THE PLACES WE CALL HOME

ANDREWS GROVE: GUILFORD TOWNSHIP

Open just about any of the Medina County history books and you'll read pages describing the lay of the land in minute detail. The lists of stones, streams and trees produce a poetry all their own. The passages written about Guilford Township were no different.

A vein of sandstone ran through the area, thickest in the northeast section of the township, and members of the Pelton family opened a stone quarry. Stonecutters sliced through chunks of it, creating foundation blocks for barns and houses in the area. Hattie M. Krout, who contributed the rural Guilford Township section of the 1948 history book produced by the Medina County Historical Society, wrote: "As the better part of the vein was worked, the trade was discontinued, and for a number of years nothing was made of it. The highway department endeavored to use this stone on the Blake northern road, but it was found to be too soft for road work, as the tires soon ground it to powder."

The sandstone walls of the "Old Maid's Kitchen" tempted generations of the younger set to inscribe their names in the soft rock. It was the site of a spring that bubbled up, also in the northeastern township quarter, a spot

that has been the gathering place for generations, when a place was required for an outing. It is known as the Petrifying Spring, and hundreds of young people used to go there in the spring and summer to gather wild flowers… The water of this spring is fine and clear at all times, and as it flows down over the hill from its source, it turns to stone leaves, sticks and bones, in fact any organic matter placed in the path where it flows. It is not frequented as much in late years, as it cannot be reached by automobile.

Andrews Grove, perched on the north border of the township, she wrote, formerly featured hundreds of large maple trees. For some it served as a sugar camp or sugar bush, buckets hung in the spring to catch the rising sap when sweet maple mists boiled up from the shacks set out in the woods. For others it became a place for church revivals, tapping into souls to distill the sweet spirit of God into faith.

In earlier days,

meetings were held there every summer. The Methodist denomination sponsored these gatherings, and crowds of pedestrians and carriages wended their way there. They came from Ashland, Wooster, Orville and other places equally distant, and nearer home as well. Tents were set up and cooking places prepared, and while some of those attending preferred to lodge with members in their homes, many remained for the two full weeks or longer in the woods.

In the late 1930s, the Reverend Wilmer Shelly, then pastor of First Mennonite Church, built a summer home in the grove. Carrying on the earlier tent meeting tradition, his congregation hosted vesper services, and "benches, a desk and an organ were placed on the lawn near his home, and the old forest again rang with the hymns of the church. Ministers of different churches were invited to participate in these services, and for many weeks until fall weather made it no longer practicable, the people came to these sunset meetings."

Vesper services ended when Shelly sold his home, but holding church outside echoed early pioneer worship, when voices lifted in prayer and song transformed any cabin or forest into a rustic parish.

SPENCER: KEEPING CHRISTMAS

In Baskin and Battey's 1881 county history, the writer reported:

Through the long winter evenings, the good-natured jest was passed around, as they cracked nuts by the side of the blazing fireplace; and the hum of the spinning wheel or the sound of the loom was heard in the cabins as the busy housewives prepared wearing apparel for their families. One industrious young woman prepared her wedding outfit by the light of the fire, to which was frequently added a pork-rind to make it burn brighter. Her people required her services during the day, and were too poor to afford her candles. But she was too plucky to despair.

They described how settlers kept the holiday, when "young people would collect on Christmas Eve and go from house to house firing guns and bidding everyone 'Merry Christmas'; they were then asked in, and treated to cakes, apples and sometimes to cider."

This same spirit infected young men with too much time on their hands when they improvised a "Chriskingle" monster from a sheet with red patches sewn on it to represent a mouth, nostrils and eyes.

One of the boys was elected to wear the contrivance. Like the gun-toting group, he and his friends visited their unsuspecting neighbors, opening doors and scaring the residents. Settlers from New England weren't acquainted with the custom, but the Dutch pioneers rewarded the mischief-makers with a chase and capture that ended in a march back to the cabin for food.

W.E. Sooy once put on the Chriskingle, and went to the window of a wagon-maker named Hayes, at the center of Spencer, who happened to be sitting facing the window, where the terrible head appeared. Sooy scratched on the side of the house to attract the attention of Hayes, who looked up, saw the red mouth, the glaring eyes, the distended nostrils and twisting and twirling horns. The sight was too much for the poor man, who with a long-drawn "Oh, God, and must I go?" fainted dead in his chair.

Sooy took to his heels, as badly scared as the wagon-maker himself, thinking he had scared the poor fellow to death, and, until he heard the wagon-maker was alive, he was rather uneasy.

A Look at Litchfield

When the Union army called for volunteers, seventy-five Litchfield Township men enlisted—about one-third of the village population. The soldiers who returned, despite their weariness, brought home a willingness to share their stories. One of these tales, retold in the 1948 *History of Medina County*, involved Captain John Radie,

who with his men had dug in on the slopes of Missionary Ridge. The Confederates discovered the Captain and another Union officer were the sole occupants of an advanced trench and in the Captain's words, "were making it damned uncomfortable for us." When the situation became unbearable, the officers decided to move into a depression somewhat further up the ridge.

They crawled over the protective edge of their pit and scrambled to their feet, making a dash for cover. Their men lying hidden on the slope saw their officers advance and rose in a body behind them. "What was a man to do?" asked the Captain. "The Rebs were raking us with their fire and it was no place to stay. I waved my sword and yelled, 'Come on boys, we'll give him hell' and we did." With a wild yell they swept up the hill. Their troops followed…The first men to reach the summit fought hand to hand for the guns, but the Southern troops were soon forced to retreat, leaving the Yankees in possession of the Ridge.

The fighting spirit wasn't limited to the battlefield. In 1862, a skirmish in the township squashed the intent of Southern supporters, the Knights of the Golden Circle, who allegedly passed information to Rebel units and shipped clothing infected with smallpox to Union troops. Litchfield men on furlough clashed with a group of Knights who muscled in on the township's Fourth of July celebration, ending in a brawl that "ran like wildfire around the square. Women joined—there was hair-pulling—and the clothing of at least two of the unwelcome visitors was so torn that it was necessary to wrap them in blankets before they could be dumped back into their wagons."

Trouble tagged along at a Union rally the following week, when the Knights, intent on revenge, tried to overpower storekeeper O.C. Nickerson. He surprised them. He grabbed his old rifle, leapt over the counter and "backed the rabble into the street and kept them covered till the last Knight was in the wagons, when they again departed from Litchfield at break-neck speed."

"As the last wagon bumped over the crossing, Nickerson dropped the butt of his rifle to the ground, remarking it was sure lucky he didn't have to shoot. The gun wasn't loaded."

In 1871, the township built a new town hall after a fire destroyed the building on the northwest side of the square, and with memories of war still fresh, they installed a marble tablet inscribed with the names of each Litchfield man who fought. It included four who died in battle and indicated that eight men suffered wounds and six died in the South from disease.

TALL TALES OF GRANGER TOWNSHIP

Granger Township, originally attached to Bath Township in neighboring Summit County, petitioned for official township status in 1820.

"They had no political clout until they became a 'real' township," said JoAnn Boruvka, one of the township historians. "They had to apply to the [county] commissioners, and they had to have chosen a name approved of by the commissioners, who would then set the date of the first election."

The first board of trustees consisted of N.A. Goodwin, S. Pauli and Festus Ganyard. John Codding was clerk, and people voted in Burt Codding as justice of the peace. The 1881 history records: "In January of 1822, the Trustees appointed Ira Ingraham as Township Constable. The first money paid into the township treasury was a fine of 25 cents, imposed upon one [of] its inhabitants for swearing."

Settlers named their new home "in honor of the former proprietor, who had become noted and distinguished as a Legislator in the State of Connecticut." Gideon Granger also served as postmaster general.

Historians laid it on thick when describing the territory:

> In natural beauty, Granger surpasses any of its sister townships by the variety of its surface. At the spring season of the year, the scenic effects of the hills and mountain knolls in the eastern part of the township are exceedingly attractive and pleasant to the eye...On one of the elevations, a half-mile east of Grangerburg, formerly stood an ancient fort...The origin of the fort is entirely shrouded in mystery, and there is nothing to indicate who were its builders and for what purpose it served.

Two early, larger-than-life pioneers—William Coggswell and his uncle, Gibson Gates—put up a hunting cabin in eastern Granger on the spot known as Porter's Pinnacle. Coggswell, not exactly a modest man, often recounted his prowess as a hunter and woodsman. "When ten years old, I was, in the absence of my father, compelled to chop and prepare fuel. I had no shoes to wear in the winter season. To keep my feet from freezing, I heated a board at the fire, carried it out, and then stood on it when chopping. When it became cold, I brought it in and heated it again, and in that way made it answer for shoes and stockings."

The intrepid Coggswell described several hair-raising encounters with bears and wildcats, like the following: "During the early settlement, there was a she-bear that annoyed the settlement by frequently carrying off hogs, calves and other domestic animals. She was often threatened, and as often pursued."

Coggswell called on Isaac Sippey for help, followed the bear's trail and also found a honey tree in the process. "We scooped out a trough with the ax, and filled it with choice honeycomb, and night coming on, encamped there, faring sumptuously on bread (which we always carried with us) and honey." So fortified, Coggswell and Sippey finally not only dispatched the bear but her two cubs as well.

It took the right stuff to be a pioneer, and *Gazette* files from 1891 yielded an article written in honor of Saloma Treman Hatch, born October 8, 1805, in Canandaigua County, New York, who settled in Granger Township with her parents when she was twelve.

"At this time, the country was dense wilderness, with not a road in the township. Her father, Jeremiah Treman, settled on the farm owned by the late Myron Sheldon in the northeast part of Granger. They lived with Ashur Welton until they could build a log house."

Six weeks later, the family hung blankets at the doors and windows to keep the worst of the cold out of their new dwelling and moved in. As in many early accounts, marauding wolves (who have always gotten bad press) "would come and howl so near that the house would fairly shake." Jeremiah Treman and brother John blazed the trees from their place to Weymouth and marked the road known as the Treman Road.

At twenty-two, Saloma married Connecticut-born Hoel Hatch. They had eight children: Hannah, Lorenzo, Nancy, Lydia, Judson, Julius, Frank and Emily. When Hoel died in 1883, Saloma moved in with her grandson, Cort E. Hatch. At the time the article was published, Saloma was eighty-six "and is remarkably smart and active for one of that age."

HINCKLEY TOWNSHIP:
BARN RAISINGS, SOCIALS AND WHISKEY

As men herded more sheep into Hinckley Township, the wolves watched with interest from the cave-riddled ledges. Judging by the stories the hunters spun—some from very thin threads of credibility—hundreds of wolves lurked in the shadows at every turn, preying on unsuspecting lambs and people caught out after dark whose imaginations filled in the blanks of belief.

History texts—especially local history—can be narrow footbridges, slippery and biased crossings from one event to the next, and the 1881 *History of Medina County* is no exception. Like a succession of cooks tinkering with an old recipe, each one shakes a little more spice into the stew.

Still, wolves aside, the rugged terrain of Hinckley Township challenged the settlers, the families who built cabins on the ridge. Men too restless to be content characters in an old New England story wanted to write their own, bringing their wives and children into the cast with them.

Nathan Damon and Jacob Shaw pulled up stakes in Massachusetts and moved to the area in 1831. They weren't alone long. Caleb Damon brought his wife, daughters and one-hundred-year-old grandmother, Lucy, the following year. Lyman and Hiram Miller, father and son, hired Asahel Welton to build their cabin while they returned to New York for their families in 1833. Welton, unable to locate the site in their absence, had to wait until they returned.

New neighbors meant cabin raisings, barn raisings and socials—and whiskey. The Hinckley Township settlers were, according to the history book, "for quite some time, during the early days, excited on the temperance questions...Whisky was in those days one of the social elements, and no public occasion was thought complete, unless there was a good supply of liquor." One group vowed not to assist at raisings if whiskey was served, and their equally determined counterparts said they wouldn't show up if the day was dry.

S.C. Oviatt, who "liked a 'drop' now and then," agreed to dispense with whiskey during a raising at his farm so the temperance men would help.

> *Craig, a rough, whisky-drinking fellow, but a man of experience in barn-raisings, "bossed" the job. After raising the bent* [part of the structure that strengthens the framework transversely], *Craig called out, "There, you cold-water cusses, hold that till I tell you to let go." They did hold till they got tired and could hold no longer, and over went the bent.*

William West jumped for it and landed safely, but the pike pole caught Robert McCloud and fractured his skull. He recovered, but the "incident rather added to the ranks of the temperance people, and a society was formed which became influential and important."

The temperance debate may have encouraged the growth of churches in the township, beginning with the Methodist society in 1822. Members met in private homes and later at the log schoolhouse whenever the circuit riders came through. Historians painted a sweet picture of four sisters who rarely missed a sermon on the ridge: "Letitia Swift, Mrs. McCreary, Mrs. Chester Conant and Mrs. David Taman, would come through the woods together, singing hymns and making them ring with their bright and clear voices. They came dressed in all the simplicity of the times; in plain sunbonnet or a bandana handkerchief answered the purpose of the fashionable bonnet today."

Eventually the ridge congregation joined the second Methodist group that met near the center, with others joining the Congregationalists. Free-Will Baptists and Disciples spread throughout the township. And one might guess that once they could afford to build their own churches, it was only the beams and bells they raised, not the tin cups of homemade hooch.

YORK TOWNSHIP: CASTLES IN THE AIR

"How precious to our happiness are the castles that we build!" wrote the authors of the 1881 county history book. "How sweet it is to let the imagination wander off into pleasing representations of future stages of life; and how universal and cherished is this phase of human character."

They referred to the settlement of York Township and the care with which pioneers chose their land. They wanted to be close to mills, quarries and good water. If a store or school was already established, so much the better.

> *If any or all of these things were yet lacking, the settler chose a home where...the farm would be favorably situated when the county became well-settled. Sometimes, as was quite often the case, the settler arrived in the wilderness with more children than dollars, trusting that with the aid of those two valuable assistants—help and self-denial—he might at last secure a home where he could pass the remainder of his days in security and peace.*

Few families initially chose York for their log cabin castles because the land cost was "far above that in neighboring townships. The price asked varied from 25 cents to $1 above the current rates, and in the estimation of a man with but little money, this was an important consideration, and effectually prevented the sale of the land." (In 1826, the acreage of York was valued at $29,936.00, and the taxes paid by Fanny Chapman, Elijah Hubbard, James Mather, Thomas Still and William N. Still totaled $295.62.)

York—so named because most of the newcomers came from "York State"—remained virtually untouched until June 1830, when George Wilson purchased a small tract of land, built a rough cabin and brought his family, who had camped on Medina's doorstep until their new home was ready. By October, Wilson had the company of Levi and Lawson Branch, Harvey Bruce, E. Munger, John Dunshee, Reuben Stickney and Solomon Hubbard.

Levi Branch brought a small stove with him from New York, an item "looked upon by all visiting neighbors as a curiosity, and was spoken of so often throughout the neighborhood that 'Branch's stove' became almost a by-word." The Branch cabin may not have had a proper roof, floor or doors, but it had a warm heart.

When asked why he built his home on the corner of his farm that was farthest removed from Medina, Branch replied that since he owned the only team and wagon during the winter of 1830–31, it gave him "the pleasure of conveying all his neighbors living on the diagonal road to church in Medina every Sunday morning."

Community-minded Branch also played a key role in the early education efforts of the township. His son, Theodore, taught the first school in one room of Levi's house until the fall of 1832, when the neighbors built a log schoolhouse. Theodore continued as teacher at least through the first formal school term.

Twenty York settlers—that included almost everyone in the township—held the first election in Levi's barn on April 2, 1832. They elected Thomas Brintnall, Sylvanus Thomas and Levi as trustees, Philo Fenn as treasurer and Alexander Forbes as justice of the peace.

Forbes, "a tall, powerfully built man," also gained fame as a skilled hunter in York. "Extravagant stories are told concerning his ability to bring in large quantities of game and his superior marksmanship. He often went into the forest in the morning and returned at night with forty or fifty squirrels…on one occasion of about three weeks, he killed eight deer, on an average, per day."

Other settlers who arrived over the next five years, all looking for exceptional locations for their own castles, had been informed that "the excellent and well-traveled Norwalk Turnpike extended through the center of the township and afforded an unparalleled outlet to market and mill." They also heard about Mallet Creek, "in whose clear waters thousands of speckled trout abounded."

In reality, the truth had been stretched like old harness leather—speckled frogs, not trout, populated the creek, and R.M. Lampson dispelled the other half of the myth when his wagon, carrying only a light load, sank to its hub in the mud of the celebrated roadway.

"This enraged Mr. Lampson, whereupon he uttered some startling truths in a peculiarly emphatic manner, respecting the famous turnpike and the meandering Mallet Creek. He and many others were for a long time singularly tender on the subjects of speckled trout and turnpikes."

HARRISVILLE TOWNSHIP: RAILROAD WAR

On the Medina County map, the lines indicating the path of the railroads look like lines of stitchery piecing the land together into a crazy quilt pattern. Towns were eager to have train service, which connected them to a wider world. Usually men armed with pickaxes and sledgehammers swaggering down the road to put down track were a welcome sight. But a November 1906

Crowds gathered to celebrate Lodi's homecoming in September 1911 (Harrisville Township). *Courtesy John Gladden.*

Gazette headline proclaimed: "Farmers in Revolt—Citizens of Harrisville Meet Railroad with Force, Clear a Public Highway of Engines, Cars and Track, and Hold the Fort Till They Win in Securing an Injunction."

The trouble started in March 1906, when township trustees R.M. Albert, J.C. Jamison and J.D. Kennard brought an injunction against the Akron & Chicago Junction Railroad Company (the B&O). "The company in building its new line through Harrisville desired to divert two roads west of Lodi and so same building an expensive overhead bridge. The citizens of Harrisville almost unanimously opposed the wish of the railroad."

The trustees stood on shaky legal ground but could not persuade the county commissioners to get involved at that point. Judge Hayden dissolved the injunction the last Friday in October

> *on the grounds that the township trustees were not the rightful parties to bring injunction proceedings, and that sufficient cause of action was not shown.*
>
> *The railroad chose its time in this case as burglars choose their time to rob when their victims are most helpless. In the gray dawn of last Sunday morning, the whole construction force...swooped down on the West Salem road and the first road north of it, about mile west of Lodi, built board fences across the highways where they wanted the change in the roads, and began erecting an embankment for their road bed.*

By Monday morning they had moved five dirt cars on a temporary track. But the company hadn't reckoned with the determination of Harrisville residents, who decided to clear the road "by any means necessary." Farmers passed the word to be at the site before daylight Tuesday morning. "And there they were, with their teams and scrapers, grim and determined. Every man believed it would probably mean force and fighting."

On Tuesday, the rail crew rushed three engines on the roadway track, jamming two of the dirt cars on the north bank of the road. The farmers threatened to use dynamite that would "send those engines skyward—and the dynamite was brought. Two engine men looked into those grim farmers' faces, saw they meant business, and abandoned the live engine."

The farm force pushed the dead engine and another dirt car into the ditch. "A dozen teams were hitched to the rails of the track, and twisted and broken, it was dragged to the roadside. The score of teams and scrapers and a hundred strong willing hands began hauling away the railroad embankment. Before noon, the traveling public was using the West Salem road west of Lodi as usual, a hundred farmers standing guard to see that it was kept open."

It was, the November 2, 1902 *Gazette* reported, "an ugly and dangerous situation, the worst that has ever imperiled the peace and order of this county. Those determined farmers were there, as they openly avowed, to die if necessary to defend their rights against a predatory corporation. And they would have done it."

Attorneys Siddall and McClure tried to convince the county commissioners to file an injunction against the railroad, while the farmers held their ground. "A tent was pitched at the roadside for a night guard, a stove placed therein, bivouac fires lighted." The tent also contained a "stack of shotguns and a good supply of dynamite; but the orders were, if a night attack came, not to use the guns, but, if necessary, cut the traces of the railroaders' teams and so render them helpless to fill in the roadway."

None of the railroad men ventured close to the "lawless mob," and while they worked a safe distance away, the company attorney appealed to Sheriff Orr "to do anything and everything to clear the public highway of the farmer mob...and let the railroad proceed with its own sweet will."

Orr, however, concluded that the citizens could protect their rights against the railroad until the court made a decision and turned his horses back toward Medina, to the cheers of the crowd.

The commissioners finally filed an injunction on Wednesday, and McClure delivered the papers to Judge Hayden, who immediately granted the injunction Wednesday evening. A second injunction by Probate Judge

Plank also was granted, and the farmers on the roadway "were glad to quit and quietly go home."

Although the railroad company brought a $5,000 suit against the farmers, it seemed few regretted their actions. They had stood up for what they believed, and that was that.

THE WOMEN OF BRUNSWICK HILLS TOWNSHIP

Back and forth, the shuttle crossed and recrossed the threads on the loom. By the sunlight streaming in the window, Meletiah Tillotson watched the homespun cloth grow slowly, inch by inch. Meletiah, better known to family and friends as Millie, allowed her dreams to grow along with it. She imagined folding the coarse homespun and packing it for the trading trip to Cleveland. As she caressed the cloth with work-roughened hands, it changed into yards of pink calico and the dress that she would cut and sew.

Homespun, she thought, was as boring and drab as a sparrow's wing. Millie wanted a dress the color of the wildflowers that grew in the fields around the cabin. If she hurried, she could get more cloth finished before her sister, Sally, came home from teaching school. She planned to wear her new dress to church so maybe Lucius Warner would take more notice of her. She'd known Lucius since 1816, when they sat in the schoolroom together.

By the time spring winds whipped through the fields, Millie found the calico, pink as the inside of a seashell—or a pig's ear. She cut and sewed whenever she could, stealing moments from making lye soap or helping her mother bake bread or scrub clothes. The women in the community frowned on the frippery, but Millie wore it to church anyway and took the scolding "for wearing such gaudy colors." And although there's no proof it was the charm of the pink dress, Millie did marry Lucius in 1828.

There always are a few people who stand out in a crowd, and that's just as true in the old history books. Maria Hulet, who dug her own well and killed a buck with an axe, is a standout. So was Rhoda Ward Stow, a widow with two grown children, Daniel and John, who came to Brunswick from Pittsfield, Massachusetts, in April 1817. She kept house for her brother, the Reverend Jacob Ward, until he returned to Massachusetts, married Lucinda Robinson and brought his new bride and his parents back with him. In turn, Lucinda accepted her role as a pastor's wife by providing meals and lodging for the circuit-riding ministers.

Mamie Grunau, president of the Brunswick Area Historical Society, thought it must have been lonely for the women, since homesteads stood so far apart. The lamps shining in neighbors' windows probably seemed as distant as stars in the night. The women did find camaraderie at church services, quilting bees and dances, but those were special occasions, and they devoted most of their days to work.

And while Millie kept a vision of pink calico in her heart as she swept and hoed and cooked, her sister Sally taught at the first school in Brunswick Hills Township. She had to keep students in line, a tough task since many of the students were probably almost as old as she was. The 1881 history stated, "Barring the teacher out was a practice not to be avoided on holidays and such occasions were relished with unbounded delight by the entire school."

When Parmelia Freese taught classes, it wasn't unusual for her father, the judge, to sit in the classroom and "impart his advice to the scholars and render any needed assistance to the teacher." But sometimes there wasn't anyone to assist them, and the women were on their own.

Jane Wilson Easton, who married Norman Chidsey, had to fend for herself and their children when Norman had to return to Pompey, New York, to bring his mother and sister to Ohio after his father died. She regularly walked five miles into Brunswick from the cabin, carrying butter and eggs to trade for tea, sugar and calico when he was away. Grunau said that Jane was skilled with medicinal herbs and, true to the pioneer spirit, helped those who were ill, even if the knock on the door came at midnight. "All she asked was time to dress and collect her herb remedies."

LOST IN MEDINA TOWNSHIP

One Easter Sunday, I walked with my in-laws through the small patch of woods on their property. Slender bramble whips snatched at our legs, and the sun cut sharp shadows from the branches where few tender leaves unfurled. A stand of wild cherry trees wore clusters of pale blossoms. The narrow yellow petal of an unidentified flower opened small starbursts of color underfoot.

The children thought the underbrush was thick, but in reality it is a mere ghost of what once sprang up across the county.

James Moore recorded the account of his initial trip to the area in April 1816, a time when Zenas Hamilton was the only permanent inhabitant in what would become Medina Township. With the help of Hamilton and other new arrivals James Palmer and Jacob Marsh, Moore raised a cabin and then, without benefit of a horse or oxen team, cleared three acres and planted them with corn before returning to Massachusetts for his family.

This covered bridged in Medina Township was one of the last in the county. *Courtesy Medina County Historical Society.*

Billy Bloomfield ran the sawmill at Weymouth, Medina Township, in 1860. *Courtesy Medina County Historical Society.*

Initially, every area he liked had been reserved, but Captain Lathrop Seymour volunteered to show him an unmarked site near his own. "Accordingly, the Captain, with tin cup, and a most formidable butcher knife, led the way, and as if by instinct, found his way some ten or eleven miles through a dense forest...we descended the branch of the Rocky River and found our way to Zenas Hamilton's, where we spent the night."

Most of the pioneers said dark things about the surrounding territory. "The woods were full of wild beasts, some of which would not hesitate to attack human beings when pressed by hunger, and if a person chanced to get lost in the forests, they ran great danger of being devoured by them."

People occasionally did wander off and lose their way, as recorded in an 1869 *Gazette* story regarding the disappearance of Lydia Marsh, written by her brother Jacob shortly after their settlement in 1816.

It occurred when Lydia was house-sitting for the Palmers, who had gone to Sullivan to assist surveyors. At dusk, one of her brothers would walk over to watch the house at night and keep her company. One evening, he encountered an empty house and barnyard. He found the milk pail hanging on a fence post, but no sign of his sister or the Palmers' cow.

Her brother hightailed it home to organize a search party. Men looked

> *through the night, between Palmers' and where Weymouth is now located...*
> *but no trace of the lost one could be discovered...it had rained in the fore*
> *part of the evening, but before midnight turned cold, commenced snowing*
> *and froze hard. We supposed she had become exhausted with fatigue and*
> *benumbed with cold, and if she had not already perished, would soon, if*
> *not found.*

Not long after a new search plan hatched, Lydia showed up "looking some years older than she did the day before, but otherwise safe and sound." She had gone after the wayward cow and out of familiar territory. Deep into the night, she stumbled onto a road but decided to wait until morning to follow it. She curled up by a big tree, "pulled [off] her stockings, wrung the water out, wrapped her feet in her clothes and awaited the coming of daylight," when she made her way to the Palmers' house with the hope of sneaking back with no one the wiser.

The writer concluded:

> *The above incident took place within a few miles of the county seat...as*
> *we look around us at the farms and pleasant homesteads, standing so thick*
> *that one may travel all day and never be out of sight of some farmhouse,*

it is rather difficult to realize all that is contained in the words "lost in the woods," and that only sixty or seventy years ago the forest was dark and almost impenetrable except to wolves, bears, panthers and other ravenous beasts, and the cabin of a settler was to be found at rare intervals.

MONTVILLE TOWNSHIP: PIONEER PROFILES

The pages at the back of the 1881 *History of Medina County* detail biographical sketches of township residents. The subjects of these little snippets paid for the privilege of being published for posterity, but when you pick through them, there's a little bit of Edgar Lee Masters's *Spoon River Anthology* feel to some of them.

In the fragile, deteriorating pages, you still can meet William, Ira, Moses, Lysander, Anthony and other dreamers—gold-seekers and farmers, carpenters, the father of soldiers, a Democrat in Republican territory—who, like the men in Masters's Illinois graveyard, now "lie sleeping on the hill."

William McDonald loved the sweep of the land and possessed "good property, on which good buildings have been erected." The eldest of nine children born to John and Rachel in 1830, he took the measure of wood with a carpenter's sharp eye. McDonald knew the measure of a man on the other side of a rifle as well, fighting in seven engagements, gone almost a year before walking back into Medina County's peace.

Ira Bennett traded a handful of nails for the teasing glitter of gold. "When 18 years of age, he began the carpenter's trade, which he followed several years, and Dec. 13, 1851, he started for the Pacific Slope, being lured thither by the gold excitement of that period. He passed two years there, with fair success, and then returned to this native county, where he has since followed agricultural pursuits."

At twenty, S.M. Thayer, son of Russell, "commenced teaching school, which he followed, during the winter season, for ten years, farming during the summer. He has resided in this township since the settlement here by his father [1833], except one year in Granger Township." Antoinette Clark, born in Medina Township to Ransom and Elizabeth in 1826, captured his heart, and they married March 22, 1848.

Their youngest child, Mary Cornelia, died in infancy, but their sons, Russell and William, survived, one stepping into the fields as a farmer, one into the classroom as a teacher, "having taken a course at the Medina Normal School." Antoinette worshipped at the Episcopal church, a neat, white frame building in Medina, on Sunday mornings, the horses and buggies tied outside. The Thayers were an upright family, and a brave one politically. S.M., who served two terms as a justice of the peace, was "a Democrat, and voted first for James K. Polk for president."

Linus, S.M.'s brother, also "commenced teaching school, which he followed for some time during the winter season." He married Charlotte Perkins, Theodore and Polly's daughter, on March 13, 1856. Unlike his brother, Linus voted a Republican ticket. His bravery shone on the battlefield when he served as a soldier in Company E, 166th Ohio National Guard. Linus also stepped up to bat for public service, taking a successful swing as "a worthy and estimable citizen" who served as township clerk and trustee.

SHARON TOWNSHIP: THE GHOST OF LOTTIE BADER

The telling of ghost stories is a campfire and Halloween tradition. A dog's howl becomes a wolf's voice, a branch scratching the porch roof becomes the scrabble of skeletal bones looking for entry.

A few houses in Medina County claim that some of their residents are of the unearthly variety, but the spirits seem to be quiet guests, sometimes mischievous, sometimes helpful, seen when least expected.

Judge Albert Munson, who believed contact could be made with the spirit world, routinely held séances in the attempt to contact the spirit of assassinated U.S. president William McKinley and others who had crossed over. He wasn't alone in his beliefs.

In their local history book, *Early Sharon Township*, Ruth Ensworth and Helen Vaughn recounted the legend of Lottie Bader, who often held séances at her

Judge Albert Munson stands on the steps of his East Washington Street home. *Courtesy Medina County Historical Society.*

family's home in Sharon Township. "Within a short time, Lottie Bader's fame spread throughout the Western Reserve."

Her fame was short-lived. When her health began to fail, she discontinued the séances. "From a remarkably pretty girl, she had become a listless, pale and emaciated creature. As her condition worsened, she made a request that she be buried near her parents' kitchen door so that she could easily visit them from time to time."

Her parents, who apparently also were spiritualists, didn't think this unusual and agreed to do so. Lottie died on July 24, 1858, during a terrible storm, but "a short time before her death, Lottie asked her mother to bring her tea and toast. When Mrs. Bader returned to the kitchen, she saw the vision of a headless woman leaning over the stove making tea."

Mrs. Bader claimed the vision told her she would have to prepare tea and toast "once a week the rest of your days." Lottie's ghost is to have roused her mother the following Friday at midnight, asking for tea and something to eat.

One evening a week for the next five years, Mrs. Bader made tea and toast and set it on the kitchen table. Each morning after, the cup was empty and the plate held only crumbs.

Most people ignored the story. They got on with their lives, going to work in field and factory, shrugging off the shiver of spirits.

Lottie's body was eventually reburied on the hilltop in the township cemetery, but of the Bader homestead Tom Hood wrote, "O'er all there hung the shadow of a fear / A sense of mystery the spirit daunted / And said as plain as a whisper in the ear—the place is haunted."

The Alderfer Crate Company once employed many Sharon Township men. *Courtesy Sharon Township Heritage Society.*

HOMER TOWNSHIP: DRIVING MISS DAISY

Come July and what seems to be the annual repaving of roads, cruising through the county is a test of vehicle maneuverability, driver dexterity and creative language arts. But pitfalls and potholes aside, streets skinned down to the cobbles give us a glimpse of horse-and-buggy days. Historians who wrote about Homer Township in the 1948 county history book measured cultural advancement by the improvement of roads.

The people of Homer Township have from the earliest days kept pace with the progress of civilization as can be seen from their roads. The first roads in the township were like those of any other place in the wilderness—merely paths cut through the forest. These trails were little better than swamps, and pools of water stood in them after every rain. The mud was thick and sticky...Finally the pioneers hit upon the idea of improving the roads by placing logs across the route, side by side. Such a corduroy road extended north from the center of Homer to LaGrange.

At that historical juncture, imagine the county spread out like a giant board game, where travelers toss the dice and draw a game card that reads: "Toll gate. Pay road repair fee and advance ten miles." "One such toll gate, which saw service for many years, stood one mile north of the village of Homerville in front of the Homer Barnes residence."

Road development continued, particularly during 1915–18, due to "an increased demand for improved highways in order that government trucks carrying war supplies could take the most direct route. By December 1918, all of the main roads were improved" including the "Benjamin Franklin Highway, commonly known as Federal Highway No. 224. Gradually the automobile brought a need for improvement of secondary roads."

G.W. Barnes and E.J. Nausel bought the first horseless carriages in Homer, purchased the same day in 1908 at Cleveland dealerships. Barnes's first car was a four-cylinder Premier Roadster, Nausel's a two-cylinder Lambert. Daisy Barnes, G.W.'s wife, didn't wait around for anyone to drive her anywhere. She was the first woman driver in the township.

WESTFIELD TOWNSHIP: LOSING STOCK

Much of the early life in Westfield Township revolved around the hotel on the west side of the square. In 1838, two years after James Whiteside finished the building, which had the LeRoy Post Office attached to it like a barnacle, Dr. Caleb Stock stepped in and kept it as a public tavern. One wintry Wednesday night, not long after Stock took over as landlord, he threw a party.

He opened the tavern to most of the neighborhood and "many others from all quarters of the township," according to the 1881 Medina County history book. The few young men not invited to Stock's shindig decided to organize a hunting expedition the same night. Despite the late hour of their return, the sounds of laughter and music still spilled out into the street.

They added their own comments to the festivity by firing their muskets five times into the cold, starry sky, then scattering. "The following Monday, an officer of the law, affectionately referred to by Westfield as a 'basswood' constable from Medina," arrested eight of the men, "who, having made music on their muskets, were thus called to account as inciters of a riot."

The officer herded Oliver Morton, David King, Henry Collier, Reuben Kinney, Calvin Kidder, N.W. Ellis, T.B. Ellis and Orrin Buckingham into his wagon. By the time the rig rolled into the county seat, only Morton, Buckingham and Kinney remained. "The other five had taken French leave at or near LaFayette Center, running off in the direction of Chippewa Lake. However, in a day or so, all were recaptured and the entire party of eight was lodged in jail."

Squire Olcott bound them over to the common pleas court, with bond set at $1,500 for each. Joshua Bailey and two other wealthy citizens furnished bail. In the week it took to sort things out, "the quiet population of Westfield had lashed itself into a state of indignation and excitement seldom seen in a community of law-abiding people."

Sentiment ran high against Stock. Westfield men and women elbowed their way into the Medina courtroom for the jury trial held in the spring of 1840:

> *The indicted parties seemed least interested in the case, for they played ball with the boys of Medina even while the trial was going on. But their defense was ably managed by Mr. Benedict of Elyria, and so plainly did he make it to appear that the alleged "riot" was merely a piece of innocent and harmless sport, that a general verdict of acquittal was returned.*

Despite the acquittal, a number of Westfield citizens held an "indignation meeting" against Stock, who, with Samuel McClure representing him, sued them for defamation and slander. David Tod, who later served as governor of Ohio, defended the people. The trial, held that fall, "resulted in a verdict of $5 for the plaintiff."

The history book doesn't record what became of Stock after that, but it appears that Morton, one of the young men he prosecuted, later became a prominent citizen in the township, including membership on the Ohio Farmer's Insurance Company Board of Directors. A biographical sketch in the 1881 history described him as "Democratic from a political standpoint, yet he has never been a radical or an extremist in his views…In theory and practice, he has been a Temperance man—has yet to drink his first glass of whisky or intoxicating liquor."

CHATHAM TOWNSHIP: OIL WELLS AND MAPLE SYRUP

Chatham Township, founded 1818, is known for its sugar bush as well as the annual Apple Butter Festival, but with more than 175 years under its belt, those are relatively recent characteristics.

If you painted a succession of historical portraits, you might begin with the little cabin built by settler Moses Parsons, whose son Holden was the first child born there. The area itself first was named Holden and changed to Chatham in 1833. Vesta Richards taught classes in her home in 1828, and Mrs. Lucinda Clapp started a subscription school in 1836 at the cost of two dollars per pupil.

Businesses catered to the needs of the settlement, with cobblers, harness makers and blacksmiths setting up shop. Permelia Ripley set up a millinery shop, while Lyman Rogers tripled as a carpenter, cabinetmaker and undertaker. Josiah Packard opened a general store in 1839 about a mile south of Chatham center on Coon Club Road. He later joined forces with his brother Jonathan in 1854 to establish the store still in existence today. Packard drove two ox teams, hauling grain and produce to Pittsburgh to barter for inventory.

Chatham has had a long association with good times and good things to eat, if you add the contributions of the Rice family, who established a dam and gristmill along the Black River in 1830, as well as Dan Fellows and Francis Shaw. Fellows ran a cheese factory east of town and Shaw sold honey by the barrel. Clem Rice, descendant of Phillip and John, sold homemade ice cream in a recreational park on what became Old Mill Road.

But it was the oil boom in the 1890s and early 1900s that garnered the most attention, with the most profitable wells capped in 1919. The first well sprouted on F.R. Shaw's farm in 1890, when a man named Getchie from Wooster used water well equipment to tap into the flow.

Chatham historian Frank Munz said that Getchie pumped the well using "horse power and a mowing machine gear. People came from all over the county to see the well and to buy oil in barrels and cans for cooking and lighting." Thirty-two more wells popped up in the general area and piped oil to Lodi, where it was shipped by rail to Cleveland refineries.

An oil well gusher in Chatham became part of the village landscape in 1918. *Courtesy Chatham Historical Society.*

An oil well worker prepares to drop nitroglycerin to "shoot a well" in Chatham Township. *Courtesy Chatham Historical Society.*

Oil wells were common sights in the fields of Chatham Township. *Courtesy Chatham Historical Society.*

A gusher on the Tom McVicker farm in 1918 drew oilmen from New York and Pennsylvania.

The History of Chatham Township recorded:

> *Everyone who owned land here hoped they would be lucky enough to get a good well. Almost every lot in town had its oil well with pumps working away... Farms were cut up and farming abandoned in many cases for the "black gold." The roads were nearly impassable—knee-deep in mud in the spring and fall, ankle-deep in dust during the summer and deeply rutted in bad weather.*

Township resident and historian Phyllis Siman said that the whole town got involved, with people taking in boarders and churches selling dinners to the workers. After a third boom, the excitement and wells tapered off, but Chatham retained prominence during World War II, when the government harvested a stand of walnut trees near Rice's dam to manufacture gun stocks.

"They even took the stumps," Siman added.

LIVERPOOL TOWNSHIP: MOSES DEMING'S STORY

The kettle steamed on the stove, and Moses Deming rose to pour the boiling water over the tea leaves in his mug, stirring in a spoonful of honey. Nothing, however, could sweeten the sadness of tea for one. Three times a widower, he waded through his grief the same way he forded rain-swollen rivers on his way to Liverpool Township in 1811. He put his head down, let the rain roll off his neck and kept moving.

Almost fifty years later, Deming wanted to preserve his life and that of those he loved on paper. He grappled with words in the way he drove his small herd of young cattle through deep spring mud on the trip south from Cleveland, grabbing them by the horns and prodding them with stout poles through heavy going.

He wrote at his kitchen table, booted feet firmly on the floor as he mapped out a history that ran parallel to Liverpool's. Steam rose from his cup as he searched for the next word. His pen talked with a comfortable scratchy voice against the paper as he wandered the road back to his parents in Southbury, Connecticut.

In the narrative *Pioneer History of Medina County* by N.B. Northrop, the son of Alma Knowles and John Deming, then seventy, described life with his parents and eight siblings in a cramped cabin on one acre of ground.

His father served in the Revolutionary War, and while he fell in step with fife and drum, Alma struggled to feed the family. John sent money home, but the Continental paper barely bought a loaf of bread.

"I can remember when turnips were our bread and meat, and if a thin slice of bread was obtained, it was luxury. It was not unusual to go supperless."

At twenty-one, Moses, who had been bound out to learn the blacksmith's trade six years earlier, worked in Waterbury, where he met his first wife, Ruth Warner.

The memory of the maid lingered while Deming roamed, trying to make his fortune through "deep snow, high waters, severe cold and mud…I came to the conclusion that if I ever intended to prosper, I must cease rambling and settle down…in due course of time, I could say I was out of debt and had some cash on hand…I visited Ruth Warner, proposed and was married to her June 1, 1802."

They settled on twenty acres of land and eventually doubled that number, but although they were out of debt, Moses wanted to wander farther afield. He sold the farm to a Yankee who paid him in wooden clocks. He started to explore his new treasures. "I assumed the responsibility of taking my own apart and examining its mysteries. I spent the main portion of the day in unfixing it and refixing it and then concluded I was prepared, after serving an apprenticeship to myself, to repair wooden clocks."

Clock sales and repairs proved a lucrative move for Deming. He returned home after six weeks on the road with $180 worth of cattle and later sold more clocks for geese and other barter before turning to the manufacture of miners' wheel heads.

Always a restless spirit, it didn't take much to persuade him in 1810 to accompany his father-in-law and a small company of men to look at land in the Connecticut Western Reserve. "Father Warner and myself were supplied with clocks, which we sold or traded as we traveled."

Deming didn't like the looks of the land around Cleveland and held out instead for the Liverpool Township farm, where he lived to chronicle a life that mirrored so much of the township's history, hiring a man to "make an opening and prepare a field to plant in corn the coming spring." He started for home March 15, noting in his journal that "nothing of import happened on my way."

Wadsworth Township: The Salt—and Coal—of the Earth

Oliver Durham and Benjamin Dean walked a deer path into the wilderness seven miles from Western Star, the nearest settlement on the township line between Wadsworth and Norton. They lashed branches together for an open-sided shelter that they used until Dean's father, Daniel, and his brother, also named Daniel, arrived on March 17, 1814. With the help of other settlers, like Basley Cahow, Indian Holmes and Theodore Parmalee, they began to build cabins.

Above: Two panoramic views taken by Captain T.D. Wolbach depict Wadsworth's Public Square in 1911. *Courtesy Wadsworth Area Historical Society.*

Right: Men stand near the furnace at the Wadsworth Salt Company. *Courtesy Medina County Historical Society.*

The trolley pulls up to the gazebo built for the Wadsworth Cornet Band in 1899. *Courtesy Wadsworth Area Historical Society.*

Captain Elisha Hinsdale started a blacksmith shop in 1817 in an area that eventually became part of Norton Township across the county line. Albert Hinsdale, the captain's only surviving son, wrote about the day their cabin was finished.

> *Our house had no chamber floor, no chimney, nor was it chinked. I remember being out in the dark the first night, and the light of the fire inside made me think of a tin lantern. We did not live very well for the first two years, but we always had something to eat...Before winter, our house was chinked and daubed; we had a puncheon floor, a stick chimney from the floor up, planed doors and glass windows (the glass brought from Connecticut).*

The settlement grew, and people started small shops in addition to farming. Levi Blakeslee ran the first tannery, driving oxen to turn the axle of the granite boulder wheel of the bark mill, with vats hewn out of whitewood. When soles wore thin or bridle reins snapped, men visited James Platt's harness and shoemaking shop. Samuel Blocker, the first tailor, charged forty-five to sixty cents for a pair of pants, and while Blocker took the measure of a man for clothes, Jacob Miller sized them up coffins. Materials remained scarce, a lack that plagued Miller's business. When Julia Loomis died in 1820, Miller had only eighteen nails for her coffin. Working by torchlight, Phineas Butler drew fourteen more from his partially built house; he had brought them with him from Onondaga County, New York.

The salt industry started in 1888, when Henry Van Campen of Olean, New York, struck a stratum of rock salt while drilling for oil. Wadsworth, later known as home to Ohio Injector and Ohio Match companies, also hosted a network of coal mines.

Veins of coal ran rich in the area, with four original mines: Humphrey & Coleman on Seth Baughman's farm; Wadsworth Coal Company on the Dormer farm; Town Line Mine in the northeast corner of the township; and Stony Ridge on Don A. Pardee's land.

When strikes slowed down business in 1876, E.G. Loomis, a local coal baron affiliated with the Coleman mine, recruited black families from rural Virginia and Kentucky as strikebreakers—something he neglected to tell the workers when he hired them. Despite the situation, they stayed—a dollar per ton was too good a wage to turn down—and the company quartered them in stockades and provided them with arms and ammunition for protection. The community within the walls endured, arranging school for their children and a church for worship.

PART V

REFLECTIONS

SOMEONE ELSE'S GREENER GRASS

In the late 1950s and early '60s, the Medina Shopping Center on North Court Street was the only plaza in the town, with the red neon lights of Woolworth's shining midway between the emerald green glow of the Fisher Food grocery sign and Marshall's Drug Store at one end and the orange W.T. Grant at the other.

At Christmas, I'd stroll with my father to Woolworth's lunch counter and order hot chocolate with real whipped cream on top, while my mother carefully squeezed the Charmin and Wonder Bread ("builds bodies 12 ways") into her shopping cart at the A&P. Santa's red velvet–cushioned throne sat on the sidewalk; if it wasn't cold, he'd hold court there. More often than not he strolled, too, dutifully stopping and leaning down to listen to children spin their wishes out of the thin air, ephemeral as the scent of peppermint that clung to his coat.

Come Eastertide, the shop windows sported the latest in straw bonnets and flowered headbands, pastel sweaters and white gloves, dainty purses with gold clasps and chain handles. The clerks at Griesinger's shoe store unboxed shiny patent leather shoes that clicked like shod pony hooves if you skipped just right on the linoleum or hardwood floors. And I seem to remember a brief fling with metal "taps" nailed to the soles of my shoes to heighten that illusion. I can only say my parents were saints.

Then there were the posters that proclaimed Medina as the sweetest town on Earth. It stemmed from A.I. Root's bees, skimming the nectar from clover and storing their dripping Midas hoard in the honeyed catacombs of their hives.

The other sweet spots in town then were Tony's Candy Kitchen and Isaly's. Tony's homemade fudge was so rich and sweet that when he passed it out from his house on Halloween, my friend Connie, who wasn't supposed to indulge in chocolate, would stop under a streetlight, rip off her mask, rummage in her bag for the dark, solid square and eat it on the spot. Isaly's claim to fame, besides its chip-chop ham (it ran neck-and-neck with Lawson's), was its strawberry pie, berries mired in a thick glaze.

It you measure those Medina years in food, we looked forward to the thin, crisp French fries at the fair and the bowls of chili steaming in the September evening. We were a pretty average little Midwestern town, with traditional church spires and a theatre that showed double features and cartoon shorts, gas stations on practically every corner that gave away dishes with every fill up, a library with a horse chestnut tree shading the stone steps and a town square with a fountain and a goldfish pond.

When you think about it, how the heck did a village smack in the midst of the Connecticut Western Reserve get a name better suited for a tale out of *Arabian Nights*?

It didn't start out as Medina, but it wasn't a plain-Jane New England name, either. Elijah Boardman originally named it Mecca, after the Arabian city known as Mohammed's birthplace. But it turned out that name already was taken. So he settled on Medina instead, celebrated for being the final

The fountain graced the park on the square in Medina for many years. *Courtesy John Gladden.*

resting place of the prophet. Maybe he studied Islam. Maybe he just liked the exotic sound of their names rolling off his tongue.

We never tend to think of our own cities and towns as exotic. We live out the cliché of looking for the greener grass someplace else. Sometimes, like humorist Erma Bombeck once observed, we discover that place is located over the septic tank. Sometimes we step outside our hometowns for a little while, only to find, like Dorothy Gale, we had everything we really needed in our own backyard. We fold the dreams like clean, old baby clothes and tuck them into a trunk or put them into the Goodwill box for someone else to cherish. But maybe we need to take a closer look at what we have and realize it's someone else's greener grass.

MARCHING ON MEMORIAL DAY

When our son Jamie was four and our daughter Jenny fourteen, we walked hand in hand down Broadway on a sunny May morning to stand in the shadow of the Congregational church—with Jim, my husband, helping Jamie perch atop the historical stone marker, it was a prime spot to watch the Memorial Day parade. Like the old song title, we love a parade—at least Jim, Jenny and I do. Jamie never has been much of a fan, even as a four-year-old.

After the last bicycle decked out in red-white-and-blue crepe paper streamers breezed out of sight, Jamie looked at me, his little eyebrows knit together in a puzzled frown.

"Where are the balloons?" he asked.

"Balloons?" I lifted him down from the stone.

"You know, like Snoopy and Sonic the Hedgehog. Like the parade on TV."

Obviously his expectations had not been met, tainted as they were by visions of Macy's extravagance, even as I told him this was not that kind of a parade.

"Why do we have it, then?"

He accepted my explanation, tailored to a small child's world, about honoring soldiers, like both his grandpas, but it didn't make up for what he perceived as lack of pizzazz—and of course Santa Claus doesn't have top billing at this one. Jamie, despite his love for other hometown functions, never acquired a love for small parades. As he grew older, he didn't care much for the large ones, either.

Each year we went and each year he protested and asked, as he explained why he doesn't like parades, a variation of the question: "Why do you like to go to the Memorial Day parade every year? It's always the same."

Above: Soldiers stand at attention on the west side of the square in Medina, circa 1915. *Courtesy John Gladden.*

Left: Ford Cannon of Medina poses in his uniform. *Courtesy Medina County Historical Society.*

The county honored war heroes at the 1907 Memorial Day celebration on the square in Medina. *Courtesy Medina County Historical Society.*

This year he stayed home, but as we walked through the soft gray morning to find a spot to watch, I kept thinking about his question. Earlier, we heard the military beat of the drums echoing down the side streets as the school bands marched to the square, an invitation to come.

Why do I like the parade so much? It's strictly small town. They don't televise Memorial Day parades—there's no commercial value—and maybe that's one of the reasons. It is a parade of neighbors and friends, and we are still small town enough that when the men and women who served march by, applause ripples down the street as they pass. We are not afraid or embarrassed to show our appreciation for the gift they have given us.

I see the men in uniform, and in my mind's eye I also see the old photographs of my father, smiling and looking strong, handsome and a little uncomfortable in his army uniform before he shipped out. Other photos reveal a young GI seated on a bicycle, smiling as he poses near a tank somewhere in the European theater. At eighty-one, he is still a strong, handsome man, quiet about most of his war memories. Qualified as a carbine and rifle marksman, he fought with Forty-fifth Field Artillery Battalion, Battery C, part of Patton's army as it made its sweep across France and into the Black Forest in Germany.

He doesn't talk much about seeing bodies still floating in the water at the Normandy landing or the leg wound he received in northern France or waking up one morning to find the man dead in the foxhole next to his. He did talk about his unit driving through Paris on its push to the south and how the liberated French lined the streets, clapping and whistling and trying to give bottles of champagne and cognac to the troops.

So when the crowds in Medina applaud as the veterans march, I remember his stories: walking in bitter winter landscapes, eating rations, looking for letters from home and finally coming home, forever changed. He packed away his honorable discharge papers, his uniform and his ribbons, ignored the shrapnel he carried in his leg and got on with living.

The photos will be Jamie's one day. He loves his grandfather very much, and I suspect that one day he will hear the drums early and walk down the street, slip into the crowd at the edge of the square and applaud as the veterans march by.

VOICES OF OLD MEDINA

This morning when the dog and I went for our walk, trees loomed out of mist that wrapped the houses in clouds and softened the sunrise sky to a pearly gray, unlike the hard gold and blue of most summer mornings. The brick house around the corner—the one like something out of a fairy tale, with its patchwork slate roof and a yard of blooming roses and dainty alyssum—looks comfortable in this setting.

And it's been a lovely season of long evening walks as well, when the sidewalks are dappled with leaf shadows that drift across our paths when the wind kicks up. As soon as the supper dishes have been washed and wiped, the towels hung to dry over the oven handle, Skittles is already nosing her leash. She barks, loudly and emphatically, to hurry me along.

We bound out the door, down the streets, not slowing much until the end of our walk past the old town cemetery next to St. Paul's, the weathered stones like chunks of sculpted moon rock shining pale and sharp against the green in the last light. Skittles's toenails click and scratch as she trots over the cement sidewalks, and my sandals scuff across older stone slabs that mark an earlier era.

The savory smell of barbecue drifts out of backyards, and fragments of the news spill from open windows. We greet people watering their impatiens or practicing the lost art of porch sitting.

In August 1906, one *Gazette* editor lamented, "The beautiful weather of the past two days is the kind that makes one hanker for the smell of the pine woods and the hum of the gentle mosquito as they are found up in the wilds of northern Michigan and Wisconsin. Nothing like the great silent wilderness to sit down and rest in."

I don't know about mosquitoes, which I think are fit only for being swatted and feeding bats and birds, but walking the old side streets away from the shopping centers' hustle and bustle can be a lot like sitting in a small patch of wilderness for those of us who like a breather from progress now and then. For a short while, we can forget the snarl of traffic on U.S. Highway 42 and instead admire the maples and horse chestnuts we pass, reminders that a little of the forest and meadow this once was is with us still, that sometimes the past and present can occupy the same space.

We stop in the gathering dusk and watch a skein of geese cross a sky now faded to the milky blue of much-washed and much-worn denim. The dark arrow of honking cacophony momentarily overpowers the whirring hum of cicadas and the crickets' trilling chirps.

It's a good time of year to slip out of houses that hold the heat at night and watch meteors illumine the sky, those brief, bright trailing sparks that carry wishes made in haste.

Sultry afternoons call for slow strolls with a bamboo fishing pole slung over one shoulder. Walking lets you dream of a picnic lunch with a red-checkered cloth spread under an obliging oak. And if early summer tempts tongues with wild strawberries ripe for the picking as you hike through a pasture, the lure of brambles heavy with blackberries belongs to August. Some things are timeless in their appeal, as evidenced in another 1906 editor's commentary.

Men display an impressive catch of fish, a pleasant way to pass a summer's day. *Courtesy Medina County Historical Society.*

A couple of our old veterans of the Civil War got to feeling quite boyish the other day and concluded to go blackberrying, as they used to do about 60 or 70 years ago. They made out to get to the berry patch all right, but were too near done up to pick any. After a good rest, one pried the other off the log with a rail and they were able to get home in time for supper. They will buy their berries hereafter.

Sometimes after our walks, we sit on the porch and listen for the voices of old Medina, like the courthouse clock chiming the hour and the half, the blaring whistle of the train, not so unlike its steam-powered ancestor, the sound of neighbors sharing a quiet laugh from their shadowed porch. And who knows, there might be voices slipping under the wind, through time, old voices maybe a little hoarse from shouting on a battlefield, speculating on whether or not the blackberries are ripe.

SHOOTING STARS

One summer, when I was eight or nine, I spent the night at my Brunswick cousins' house. It was still "country" where they lived, with no competing glow from streetlights or shopping malls, so when Uncle Jim took us out into the backyard to watch an orbiting satellite cross the sky, you looked up at a sweep of black velvet still thick with stars.

Aside from a few excited comments when we spotted it, there was no sound but the crickets and our own breathing, and finally Aunt Joan's voice spilled out into the yard with a rush of light from the breezeway, calling us in to bed, breaking the spell.

It was one of those memories you tuck away, one that surfaces at odd moments ever after, and it came swimming to the dock when I discovered old *Gazette* stories about sky-related phenomena. The first detailed the course of a meteor that sizzled through early autumn skies over northern Ohio in 1899, and the second was an account of the Leonid meteor showers later that same year.

Whereas our night was one of quiet fire, the meteor came with sound effects.

"The *Gazette* last week briefly noticed a peculiar rumbling and vibration plainly heard and felt in this vicinity about 4 o'clock in the afternoon of last Wednesday. The noise resembled that of a succession of heavy explosions, and was heard by people from a region near Dayton to Lorain, at least, and perhaps beyond these points."

Writers speculated this was caused by "a detonating meteor, which came into contact with the earth's atmosphere, traveling at the rate of 30 miles a second…and the pieces of meteoric rock found in several places (one on the Aikins' farm in Royalton) were the results of heat and pressure caused by the air's resistance against the swift-rushing mass."

Of the Leonid shower, which promised to be spectacular that particular year, the *Gazette* staff felt that if the sky was clear, it was "probable that most of the population of this town, as in other places, will spend much of the night in watching the heavens. From the present estimate it may be expected that the showers will reach a maximum at 1 a.m. on the morning of Nov. 15."

Conjure up a vision of turn-of-the-century Medina County villages at midnight. The streets are dark, and for the most part the houses are, too, with perhaps a few oil lamps glowing in some of the windows. It is quiet, with just a small wind walking through the bare-branched trees, and the only true light is starlight.

Up and down the streets, doors open and close, letting out little whispers of cats, sleepy children being half-carried down the steps and people who, during normal hours, are homemakers and bankers and grocers, teachers and merchants, lawyers and doctors, farmers and harness makers.

It is cold, so they are bundled in shawls, coats and scarves. They stand on the lawns and the village greens like great night-blooming flowers, faces upturned, waiting. When the first shooting star sparks through the sky above the church spires, they will sigh and murmur to one another. Parents will tell their offspring that this will be something to remember all their lives.

"The meteorites will touch the atmosphere of the earth and become ignited by the rapidity of their flight. Countless millions of them will fall and they will appear red, white, orange, green and all the colors of the rainbow."

The *Gazette* reported, "The phenomenon of a great meteorite shower is generally a perfectly noiseless one," setting the stage by quoting Professor Harkness of the U.S. Naval Observatory's astronomical department.

> *When the streak is first formed it is narrow and perfectly straight, but it soon becomes serpentine and assumes an irregular figure, as it drifts along under the influence of wind currents in the upper region of the atmosphere. These streaks or tails are of various colors, owing partly to the composition of their elementary substances and partly to their altitude. Some are of a delicate greenish hue, while others light up the skies with a ruddy glow. Streaks of orange, red and white, with bluish white, commingle to form a most remarkable and beautiful spectacle. Occasionally, an orange-colored meteor may be observed leaving in its wake a streak of green.*

Imagine that.

MEET ME AT THE COUNTY FAIR

In August 1898, preparations for the fifty-third annual fair were underway, grown from "a mere cattle show" held on Public Square in 1839 to a thriving event noted for "the absence of gambling dens or games of chance. The society has taken a bold and determined stand upon this question and will admit nothing to its grounds known to be of questionable nature."

I haven't discovered when the first games were permitted, but "chance" describes them well, since they offer the chance to lighten your wallet as well as the opportunity to impress that special girl and win her the largest stuffed dog on the planet.

But the fair is about chances—to win blue ribbons for fancy chickens or plump pumpkins, to eat all the stuff your mother tells you not to any other day of the year, to ride the Ferris wheel after dark, swinging above the lighted, living patchwork below.

People have been taking chances since the fair was an informal exhibit of needlework in the basement of the old Congregational church. If you wanted to show off your livestock, you just showed up with it in tow—"Indeed, all that was necessary to be done was to get the stock upon the grounds. At this time nothing was known of stock classes; neither were the exhibitions made for the premiums, for none were offered. The first premiums were offered at the annual meeting in 1848," and in 1898, tickets cost two bits each or five for a buck.

Members of the Sharon Just-A-Meres 4-H Club took their projects to the fair in 1922. *Courtesy Sharon Township Heritage Society.*

I've had a soft spot in my heart for the fair ever since a family friend hoisted me to the warm, satin-smooth back of a 4-H pony, ever since I won my first blue ribbon in the junior art classes, ever since my husband leaned over the rear end of the horse I was grooming and asked me out on our very first date.

The fair gave me, and lots of other kids, a first taste of independence. My dad, on his way to work, dropped me off at the main gate before 7:00 a.m., when the grounds were quiet and empty of people except for those of us tending animals or selling breakfast to the early birds. With a few crumpled dollar bills shoved in my pocket, I headed for the 4-H barns where, when we weren't cleaning stalls or scrambling to get ready for our shows, the favorite pastime was "let's throw the club officers into the manure pile." Well, it did assure you a clear path up the midway and quick service at the food concessions.

Long before I owned a horse, the fair was the place to find the equines that galloped through my dreams—riding horses, draft horses, racehorses.

There is nothing quite like a nighttime harness race when you're nine years old and horse crazy. Drivers in their bright silks sit the sulky like gemstones in a ring, feet braced against the shafts, arms outstretched. Sulky wheels spark back the track lights, and on chilly nights the steam rises from hot coats and swirls into wispy clouds that trail in their wake as they walk back to the stables.

Before there were organized harness races, farmers pitted their horses against each other in matches at the county fairgrounds. *Courtesy John Gladden.*

During the first few fairs, "each horse ran his course alone and his time was taken and recorded by the judges," and the fastest time won, just as the draft horse "able to draw the heaviest stone boat loaded with stone was the best horse. In this way, any scrub animal, if he possessed the requisite strength, could claim the day's honor…A prize was also offered for the best lady equestrian rider which aroused great rivalry among the lady lovers of horseflesh."

I like county fairs because when you get past the flash and glitter of the midway and the rides, they are so much more. County fairs are a reminder of our ties to the earth and to our communities, descendants of medieval festivals and gatherings—and more ancient rites—celebrating harvest and life.

If you've become a little jaded, a little disenchanted, take the time to look with a child's eye again, when you held your parents' hands and walked through the barns, rode your first pony, let sticky cotton candy melt on your tongue and candy apples crunch sweet and slightly sour flavors together with each bite.

Think about the farmers who baled the sweet hay under a shimmering hot July sky, who straightened to stretch their backs and remove their hats to wipe their brows after hoeing long rows of vegetables. Remember women in berry-stained aprons who leaned over stoves in sweltering summer kitchens and put up the blue-ribbon jellies and jams; remember deep winter evenings when old hands made bright bird-track stitches across the snow of a white tablecloth or knitted a blanket for a new grandchild.

Remember the 4-Her who gave his horse a loving pat on the neck on their way out of the show ring, even if they didn't get a ribbon; the look on the face of a child seeing a black-faced lamb for the first time; the couple strolling out the gate, oblivious to the crowds, a silly stuffed dog that cost a lot of chances tucked tenderly in their arms.

HOUSES OF WEYMOUTH

Weymouth Community Church hasn't changed much since I memorized Bible verses in Sunday school class there. Neither has the surrounding neighborhood. Bypassed by the newer state route, the quiet days I remember from childhood hang on.

To reach the house in which I first lived, you drove the smooth black asphalt of Weymouth Road that ran north out of Medina and curved through the little village. A rougher road took you past the white clapboard church with its sturdy, square bell tower.

You turned left on Frantz Road, past the field behind Scandlon's house on the corner, to the first house on the right. Tires crunched on a gravel drive flanked by a few maples and some tall pine trees whose branches swept the ground like long, rustling skirts.

Built almost one hundred years ago on a grassy knoll amid the maple leaves' green whispers, the house was a plain study in wide white boards with a tin roof the color of ripe apples. A galvanized metal milk box sat next to the wide stone steps leading to the front porch, where a wooden swing, its chains chiming softly, swayed in the breeze. Grandma often sat there to shell peas. She popped each pod between her thumb and forefinger to send a small avalanche tumbling ping-ping-ping into a chipped blue enamel pan cradled in her lap. Sometimes she'd give me a handful, and I'd sit on the top step and eat them one by one to savor the crunchy sweetness.

A wooden screen door opened into the living room, where sunlight spilled through white-curtained windows and warmed the pegged floor and pale walls. The rest of the house was a concoction of oddly placed rooms.

I liked to trace the bumpy stucco wall, its prickly swirls and hollows resembling cake frosting, with one fingertip. At night, mice scurried deep inside those walls. Moths fluttered against the screens in delicate drumrolls, their translucent wings looking like petals from the massive snowball bush that flanked the porch. Crickets chirped a counterpoint from the shadows.

Like a magician whisking away a black scarf, morning changed everything. The path from the kitchen door led down a gentle slope to the giant lilac that shaded the sandbox and smothered my swing set in its luscious purple perfume. The dainty, tiny trumpet-shaped flowers felt silky in your palm. They were as smooth as the pussy willows sprouting near the creek that trickled a hard stone's throw beyond Grandma's garden patch, where she dug carrots and beets out of the crumbly earth and carried them to the cistern. The iron pump handle left a gritty residue on your hands, but if you pumped hard enough, a spurt of rusty water cleared to a steady stream that washed the dirt from the vegetables.

I'd carry them to the kitchen and sit at the table, elbows propped on the slick yellow oilcloth, and watch my mother cook. The kitchen was the best place to be when a storm blew in, but it was fun to go up to the attic to listen to the rain pelt the tin roof.

If the electricity failed, my mother lit the hurricane lamps. The sulfurous scent of a match strike lingered while she settled the glass chimneys in place, her hands like the wings of birds pressed against the fragile ark of fire. In light like that, you could feel safe.

I write about Weymouth, but this same scene took place in countless crossroads and villages throughout the county. The memories are common to us, even if the locations vary. Wherever you lived, you walked to the mom and pop grocery (gas pumps out front) to get an extra loaf of bread, shared pigs-in-a-blanket supper at the church fundraiser and, after romping in a small mountain of autumn leaves you raked, watched your father touch a match to the pile and let your dreams drift upward with the smoke.

ACKNOWLEDGEMENTS

This book would not have been possible without the assistance of many people.

Gazette publisher George Hudnutt graciously allowed the use of the "Time Frames" columns originally written for the *Medina County Gazette*. *Gazette* coworkers who have encouraged or edited my work include Liz Sheaffer, John Gladden, David Giffels, Bill Canacci, Hilary Bernstein, Kristen Nowak Winn, Rena Koontz, Terri Hinderman, Shirley Ware, Bridget Commisso, Wayne Workman, Betty Szudlo, Rick Noland, Albert Grindle, Brian Dulik, Brad Bournival, Pam Coleman and Mike Patti, with special thanks to Nancy Grubb, Rob Briggs, Heather Koorey and Cindee Tyree—and to all the *Gazette* readers who love local history.

Thanks to my parents, Frank and Gerry Setzko; the late Bess Vanaman, who first encouraged me to write; Tess Kindig, Nancy Peacock and Janet Griffing, who encouraged me to write for newspapers; Sandy Fahning, Kathryn Popio and Betty Wetzel for their expert ears at our monthly writers' critique group; and Medina County District Librarians Kathy Petras and Liz Nelson.

Thanks to my husband, Jim, and children, James and Jennifer, for their patience while I wrote "just one more sentence"; to the generosity of the Medina County Historical Society, especially curators JoAnn King and Tom Hilberg; and the township historical societies of Chatham, Hinckley, Spencer, Litchfield, Brunswick, Wadsworth, Westfield, Liverpool, Guilford (Seville), Harrisville (Lodi), Sharon, York and Granger.

And many thanks to Hannah Cassilly, Ryan Finn and the staff at The History Press.

BIBLIOGRAPHY

Cavin, Lee. *There Were Giants on the Earth.* Seville, OH: Seville Chronicle Press, 1959 and 1970.

Centiseptiquinarian Committee, comp. *The History of Chatham Township.* Chatham, OH: Centiseptiquinarian Committee, 1993.

Ensworth, Ruth, and Helen Vaughn. *Early Sharon Township.* Sharon Center, OH: Sharon Township Heritage Society, 1981.

Gazette (Medina County)

Medina County Historical Society. *History of Medina County.* Medina, OH: Medina County Historical Society, 1948.

Northrop, N.B. *Pioneer History of Medina County.* Medina, OH: G. Redway, 1861.

Perrin, W.H., J.H. Battle and W.A. Goodspeed. *History of Medina County and Ohio.* Chicago: Baskin & Battey Historical Publishers, 1881.

ABOUT THE AUTHOR

Judy A. Totts lives in Medina County with her husband, Jim, and two children, James and Jennifer. She has written "Time Frames," a local history column for the *Gazette*, for fifteen years. In 2007, she received the Northrop Heritage Award from the Medina County Historical Society, of which she is a member, for her contributions to local history. As a features writer and columnist, her work has been recognized by the Associated Press of Ohio and the Religion Newswriters Association.

Please visit us at
www.historypress.net